O'Donnell + Tuomey

O'Donnell + Tuomey
Selected Works

Sheila O'Donnell and John Tuomey

With essays by Hugh Campbell and David Leatherbarrow
Foreword by Tod Williams and Billie Tsien

Princeton Architectural Press, New York

Published by
Princeton Architectural Press
37 East Seventh Street
New York, New York 10003

For a free catalog of books, call 1.800.722.6657.
Visit our website at www.papress.com.

Photo credits
John Searle: pages 2, 22–26, 28–31, 35, 39, 70, 72–75
Helene Binet: pages 3, 41–45, 47, 49, 51, 55, 175
Dennis Gilbert/VIEW: pages 4–5, 7, 71, 77, 79–80, 84–85, 89– 91, 94, 97–99,
102–03, 113–15, 117, 129–31, 134–35, 137, 143–47, 149, 152–53, 156–59, 161,
165–67, 169–74
Bill Hastings: pages 21, 52, 54
Peter Cook/VIEW: page 37
Christopher Hill: pages 57–59, 61, 63
Ros Kavanagh: pages 100–01, 105, 107, 111
Paul McCarthy: page 192

Editing: Nicola Bednarek
Design: Deb Wood

Special thanks to: Nettie Aljian, Sara Bader, Dorothy Ball, Janet Behning, Becca Casbon,
Penny (Yuen Pik) Chu, Russell Fernandez, Peter Fitzgerald, Sara Hart, Jan Haux,
Clare Jacobson, John King, Mark Lamster, Nancy Eklund Later, Linda Lee,
Katharine Myers, Lauren Nelson Packard, Scott Tennent, Jennifer Thompson,
Paul Wagner, and Joseph Weston of Princeton Architectural Press
—Kevin C. Lippert, publisher

Library of Congress Cataloging-in-Publication Data
O'Donnell, Sheila, 1953–
  O'Donnell + Tuomey : selected works / Sheila O'Donnell and John Tuomey ; with
essays by Hugh Campbell and David Leatherbarrow ; foreword by Tod Williams and
Billie Tsien.
      p. cm.
  Includes bibliographical references.
  ISBN-13: 978-1-56898-601-2 (alk. paper)
  ISBN-10: 1-56898-601-7
  1. O'Donnell + Tuomey—Themes, motives. 2. Architecture—Ireland—20th century.
3. Architecture—Ireland—21st century. I. Tuomey, John, 1954– II. Campbell, Hugh,
1965– III. Leatherbarrow, David. IV. Title. V. Title: O'Donnell & Tuomey. VI. Title: O'Donnell
and Tuomey.
  NA997.O35A4 2006
  720.9415'09041
                                                                    2006013459

Contents

Foreword

TOD WILLIAMS AND BILLIE TSIEN

There is a sternness, a kind of sobriety that characterizes the work of O'Donnell + Tuomey. It lies in the restraint and discipline with which each project is approached, considered, and built. Their early work has a deeply ethical basis—from the choice of assignment, to the commitment to program and place, and always to building well. Their work has been deeply grounded. Their buildings feel "correct"—or in a way, inevitable. It is as if they have always been (or should have been) there. Their architecture is done without sentimentality but with a clear sense of care that verges on devotion. All this remains true of their work today.

More recent designs reveal a confidence that allows them to move into a new realm. Even as their architecture feels connected to a place, it evokes sharp, small shivers of surprise. One senses an undercurrent of shy wildness that emerges—rules broken that celebrate the discipline of the whole by contrast. Their work now has roots and wings—a sense of gravitas and a sense of rebellion; rationalism punctuated with emotion.

The windows that suddenly splay out of the rounded corner of the Glucksman Gallery are a gentle revelation. It is true that the forms can be seen as an extension of the lines in the plan, but the choice to clad them in metal breaks them out and away from the building's body. The gallery is simultaneously lifting off as it is tied down. The wooden benches, although elegant and refined, both adorn and transgress the stately limestone gallery they created for the Press Reception Room at Leinster House. Like a flock of birds that will suddenly take flight, they stand on the steps reminding us of what is permanent and what is transitory. The rectangular opening above the dining table in the center of the Howth House marks and disrupts the locus and most important space in the house. Even as you look down at your meal and around at family and guests, you are prompted to look up and acknowledge the powers above.

There is a unique syncopation between thought and intuition. The original voice of O'Donnell + Tuomey's work is found in the interplay between these two strengths—propriety and impropriety. Propriety is meant in the sense of correctness, aptness. Impropriety is found in the subtle bursts of sensuous will. Does this courage to dance between the two come from living in a new, more serene Ireland, from the freedom of children grown, or from the recognition that one's time is finite and life must be lived and celebrated if we are to leave a true mark? The work of Sheila O'Donnell and John Tuomey speaks to our mind and sings to our heart. They are serious architects. They are poetic people.

Preface

This book begins with our first public commission, the Irish Pavilion designed in 1989 for the 11 Cities/11 Nations exhibition in the Netherlands, and one of the last projects included is Ireland's Pavilion at the Venice Biennale in 2004. In the fifteen-year timeline between these two temporary constructions our work has circled around topics of culture and dwelling, with schools and colleges, art centers, and houses among our projects. While we believe that the scope of an architect's practice must encompass critical questions of strategy, the scale of our buildings has necessarily been small and specific.

The path of our practice has led to a number of different one-off designs, a series of buildings tailor-made to suit specific sites and circumstances. However, we have always thought of the work as a single project, a sustained investigation into the place-making significance of form. Amid the proliferation of building that floods over old distinctions between cities and countryside, filling up the physical space around us, works of architecture might be looked to as evidence of resistance; as counter-projects they draw attention to what is owed to the culture and what could be imagined to be of enduring value in future use. Within the limits imposed by prevailing circumstances, well-designed buildings restructure our reading of the world in the same way that a poem can offer some shape out of the confusion of practical reality.

We returned to Ireland from London as young architects in search of the soul of Irish architecture, but what we found was actually another way of looking. Instead of coming up with tangible answers to elusive and in any case misguided questions, we realized our sense of purpose through the process of the search itself—a life's work discovered in a day's work. We do not think of our buildings as separate objects to be looked at, but rather as places to see into and out from, closely related to the spaces in between and the wider world beyond—the convergence of city lanes in the Irish Film Centre courtyard in Dublin's Temple Bar, the hillside settlement of Ranelagh School, sheds crouched under the mountains in Connemara in the Furniture College at Letterfrack, campus-to-river connections in the Glucksman Gallery parkland at the University College Cork.

We hope that our buildings would feel strangely familiar in the places where they are sited and to the people who live with them. They should seem strange because they are new, because they are not completely conventional, and because they have a compressed quality that is the result of concentrated thought. They ought to be familiar in the sense that they belong where they are built, that they recast existing conditions in a new light, and that they extend or consolidate the urban and landscape systems that surround them. We have had the good fortune to work in situations where solutions could be envisaged from a consideration of the context. We intend our work to reveal rather than obliterate the possibilities that might have been latent on the site before we started.

But this perception should not be restricted only to *thereness*, to the presence of the building. Architecture's scope goes beyond that of site-specific sculpture. The question of use is crucial to the meaning of architecture, and the social assimilation of structures into the life of human beings is an essential ingredient of its value. A good building is enhanced by use and usefulness, and the pattern of its use has to be imagined in the design on the drawing board if any resonance is to be expected from its application in reality. Life often conspires against our best intentions, and frustration surrounds us in our work, but a lived-in building, which is loved in use, reminds us of the worth of an architect's effort and makes us, in turn, feel useful. In this sense, useful means more than just functional, and a strange element of the immeasurable is admitted when we take into account both mechanical operation and psychological satisfaction. A new building feels familiar if a recognition of the old world outside itself is included in its newness; if the legibility of its organization can be intuited by your feet telling you where to go rather than your conscious mind looking for signs to follow.

The ideal of building that we have been seeking is one that can consolidate and transform both situation and purpose. This is a poetic task for architecture, but its heft and its urgency are of a civil kind, pertaining to ordinary life and responding to social occasion. Grounded in the everyday, we still seek the sublime in architecture. One meaning of sublime is that which is just under the skin, and we start our search there.

Continuity and Renewal in the Work of O'Donnell + Tuomey

HUGH CAMPBELL

The story of the past two decades of Irish architecture cannot be told without O'Donnell + Tuomey. They are central characters in the narrative. Rather than being seen as an entirely separate enterprise, the development of their architecture is best understood in the context of the broader cultural and societal shifts in Ireland during the period. Founded in an era of recession and inactivity, the practice now finds itself achieving eminence in a prosperous and dynamic European nation. But while Ireland's transformation has been remarkable for its rapidity, O'Donnell + Tuomey's work has developed at a more deliberate, reflective pace.

In a recent essay, John Tuomey wrote that "Continuity and renewal is the task of architecture."[1] Indeed O'Donnell + Tuomey's work can be characterized as an ongoing negotiation between these twin imperatives. The same two themes of continuity and renewal have been central to the recent history of Irish society. The anthropologist Clifford Geertz argues that any newly independent nation must negotiate a path between what he terms "essentialism" and "epochalism," the former denoting a strict adherence to some shared culture and the latter the conscious embrace of the spirit of the age.[2] Certainly, these two forces were pervasively at work in the early years of the independent Ireland, informing every aspect of political and cultural life, but a similar dialectic has also been apparent in more recent times.[3] Accordingly, Ireland's rapid rise in prosperity has engendered worries about the abandonment of strong social bonds in favor of an unquestioning materialism; the liberalization of social policy has been accompanied by concerns about a perceived decline of public morality; and the rapid pace of development has raised worries about the fate of Ireland's urban and rural environment. In every arena, the need to move forward is accompanied by a concern about what is being left behind. Neither is this simply a matter of nostalgia or conservatism. The wish to assert and hold on to a particular Irish identity in the context of rapid modernization is more often expressed as a progressive, rather than a conservative, impulse. In the field of architecture, this is certainly the case. In fact, it is precisely through a sustained engagement with its own context that Irish architecture has discovered its own progressive, contemporary idiom.

Introducing his concept of "critical regionalism" in the early 1980s, Kenneth Frampton quoted Paul Ricoeur:

> Thus we come to the crucial problem confronting nations just rising from underdevelopment. In order to get on to the road toward modernisation, is it necessary to jettison the old cultural past which has been the *raison d'etre* of a nation?...

Whence the paradox: on the one hand, it (the nation) has to root itself in the soil of its past, forge a national spirit, and unfurl this spiritual and cultural revindication before the colonialist's personality. But in order to take part in modern civilisation, it is necessary at the same time to take part in scientific, technical, and political rationality, something which very often requires the pure and simple abandonment of a whole cultural past. It is a fact: every culture cannot sustain and absorb the shock of modern civilisation. There is the paradox: how to become modern and to return to sources; how to revive an old, dormant civilisation and take part in universal civilisation.[4]

Frampton extended Ricoeur's argument, which has clear echoes of Geertz, into architecture, discovering in figures as diverse as Alvaro Siza and Tadao Ando a capacity simultaneously "to become modern and to return to sources." He identified an architectural approach that strove to reconcile the essential and the epochal. This was, at least in part, a reaction to the increasingly trite universalism of the international style on the one hand, and to postmodernism's increased reliance on applied symbols rather than substance on the other hand. Between these poles, Frampton proposed an architecture that both derived from and communicated the specifics of place, context, environment, and tradition: an architecture that was responsive and expressive.

Frampton was part of a constellation of influences that shaped the architectural thinking of John Tuomey and Sheila O'Donnell after their graduation from college in the late 1970s. The influence of James Stirling, with whom they worked on the Staatsgalerie in Stuttgart (1977–83), helped to temper their deep appreciation for the "heroic period" of modernism with a concern for context and the use of historical precedent. Leon Krier's championing of the historic urban quartier and Aldo Rossi's exploration of enduring urban typologies contributed to their determination to re-engage with the Irish urban context after their return from London to Dublin in 1981. Although touched relatively lightly by the excesses of 1960s development, Ireland's capital had nonetheless become a site of widespread neglect and dereliction. Its future seemed uncertain, subject to the whim of politicians and road engineers rather than to any considered planning strategy. In tandem with a number of other young practitioners, including Gerry Cahill, Paul Keogh, and Derek Tynan, among others, O'Donnell and Tuomey began to argue for the validity of a living city—a place where people could live and work, a place whose historic grain and pattern should be respected and which could in turn sponsor a new kind of urban architecture. Following Colin Rowe and Fred Koetter's interpretation of the Nolli map of Rome in *Collage City*, they considered the city as both figure and ground, with built fabric and public space claiming equal importance. It was the role of architecture to repair and extend the urban realm by respecting its underlying rules and existing form.

The lessons of this early period are clearly evident in the practice's first major project, the Irish Film Centre in Temple Bar (completed 1992). The center knits seamlessly into its urban context, adapting the two main rooms of an eighteenth-century Quaker meeting house as movie theaters and establishing a new central space and route through the urban block. Existing and new architectural elements are brought together into a single ensemble. In Rossi's terms, the old meeting house becomes a "propelling" element in the city by being pressed into new formal relationships and used for new purposes. "Instead of considering time as divided in linear chronological art-historical categories, with old buildings suspended in a petrified past and new buildings projected in a volatile future, we prefer to think of all buildings co-existing in the context of the living present," writes John Tuomey.[5] The practice's subsequent work in the Temple Bar area extends and develops the same approach. As part of Group 91,[6] they were responsible for a new masterplan that, instead of the large-scale demolition and redevelopment previously proposed, envisioned a new urban quarter where existing patterns of gathering and movement would be affirmed and intensified. The historic fabric would be retained, repaired and reinforced by the creation of a series of new buildings and spaces. Similarly, the existing cultural activities in the area would become the foundation for a new group of institutions, among them the Gallery of Photography and the National Photographic Archive (both completed 1996). The gallery's large window reveals its contents to the public square it borders in a framed *tableau vivante* while offering an elevated vantage point to its visitors. In what would become a recurring concern in O'Donnell + Tuomey's work, a sense of mutuality and continuity is thus established between the everyday world and the world of the institution.

It is hardly an exaggeration to claim that the revitalization of Temple Bar changed the future of Dublin. While the area itself may have become a victim of its own success—host to too many visitors and not enough residents—its underlying ethos of urban renewal has informed the subsequent redevelopment of many other parts of the city and served as a model for similar projects elsewhere in Ireland and throughout Europe. It helped also in assuring the capital a central place in the nation's evolving self-image.

Of course, the more usual source of that self-image had hitherto been rural Ireland. In his 1987 publication *A Lost Tradition*, Niall McCullough provided an exhaustive catalogue of the indigenous built forms that inhabit that landscape—the tower houses and round towers, the cottages and grand houses, the farm-buildings and hay-barns.[7] In many respects the book was merely the latest manifestation of a tendency among Irish artists to celebrate the rural vernacular, which dated back at least to the mid-nineteenth-century archaeology of Samuel Ferguson. But for the architects of O'Donnell and Tuomey's generation it provided both a fresh invitation to "live back into the country you live in"—as Ferguson himself had put it—and a ready-made repertoire of forms with which to do so. The enduring typologies catalogued by McCullough were recognized for their capacity simultaneously to stand out from, and belong to their setting. Their prismatic clarity offered the prefect antidote to the raw ugliness of large single houses and factories that were becoming an increasingly common presence on the Irish landscape. While this re-engagement with tradition produced its share of stilted reiterations of familiar forms, O'Donnell + Tuomey quickly moved beyond imitation toward thoroughgoing reinvention.

At Blackwood Golf Centre (completed 1994) the string of simple one- and two-story volumes evokes memories of farmyards and barns without ever resorting to mimicry. The bricolage of materials and fragmented forms is also reminiscent of W. R. Lethaby's All Saints' Church at Brockhampton, and indeed the project shares some of the arts-and-crafts movement's capacity to recast the vernacular as avant-garde. In the Letterfrack Furniture College (2001) the same mode of formal reinvention has a greater seriousness of purpose. This former industrial school, with its attendant memories of repression and cruelty, is divested of its hostile aura and determined symmetry to become part of a picturesque assemblage of forms. In place of a mute, forbidding presence at its center, the village of Letterfrack acquires an articulate, legible core. Using Rossi's terms again, a "pathological" element may be said to have become a "propelling" element. A moribund institution is brought to unexpected new life.

What is also notable in the work at Letterfrack is a more pronounced interest in materials and making. There is a viscerality to the robust timber and concrete finishes that strikes a new note in the practice's work, equivalent to the gradual loosening and thickening of brushstrokes that often mark a painter's development. The clarity and directness of the construction seem to tap into the essential qualities of the wild surroundings and contribute to the sense, once again, of a vernacular being reinvented. In their presentation of this building for the Venice Biennale in 2004, the architects emphasized the importance of its material qualities by redeploying many of its key details and junctions as exhibition stands.

The "Scary House" element of this installation drew attention to another key aspect of O'Donnell + Tuomey's work—its expressive and narrative qualities. In its form and construction, the Scary House refers back to one of the practice's earliest projects—a temporary pavilion built to house the emotive paintings of the Irish artist Brian Maguire. The structure led the visitor through a complex series of spaces, each the setting for a single painting. The architecture sought to establish moods and engender emotions—it was not content to be a neutral backdrop. The Scary House continues this exploration of how spatial experience can produce feelings—in this case feelings of trepidation and unease. While their role as exhibition pieces explains the particular emphasis on dramatic communication in these two pavilions, it is notable that their architecture communicates its message through the geometric manipulation of simple construction rather than the more usual theatrical devices of lighting or "dressing." The drama is in its bones.

The generous articulacy of construction that is a constant in O'Donnell + Tuomey's work means that the buildings always speak specifically of their genesis. In fact, it seems to be by means of this insistent revelation of their own making that they acquire a greater immediate power as communicative forms and spaces. Thus, the precarious poise of the main cantilevered volume of the Lewis Glucksman Gallery (2005) is *understood* as a direct consequence of the position, rhythm, and size of the supporting concrete columns, but is *felt* as a dramatic leap from the high ground towards the surrounding treetops and the river beyond. As the architects' formal and spatial language becomes freer and more expressive, it is balanced by an increased precision of planning, construction, and detailing. Here is sophisticated, complex, and resolutely contemporary architecture that nonetheless exerts a direct and vivid impact on its occupants, and which seems to inspire a sense both of ownership and belonging. What is particularly noteworthy is that this widespread acceptance and admiration is achieved not through any pandering to popular taste or "dumbing-down" but rather through a sustained focus on the business of making architecture. The Glucksman is an almost defiantly literate building, steeped in lessons learned from Le Corbusier, from James Stirling, Alvaro Siza, Carlo Scarpa, and many others. The architects understand that, in the end, all that informs architecture—the site, the client, the economy, the culture—must be resolved through the architecture itself, but addressing those wider concerns never becomes an evasion or distraction. In an interview with the *Guardian*, the novelist Philip Roth said:

> My interest is in solving the problems presented by writing a book. . . . The crude cliché is that the writer is solving the problem of his life in his books. Not at all. What he's doing is taking something that interests him in life and then solving the problem of the book—which is, how do you write about this? The engagement is with the problem that the book raises, not with the problems you borrow from living. Those aren't solved, they are forgotten in the gigantic problem of finding a way of writing about them.[8]

But, absorbed as they are in the "gigantic problem" of making good buildings, O'Donnell + Tuomey have never lost sight of the culture within which they operate. The increasingly high profile of architecture in Ireland, and of the work of Irish architects internationally, owes much to them. To link their development to the trajectory of Irish society over the past two decades is not to confine them to narrow national boundaries, however. Ireland's own reinvention has been as much about looking outward to Europe and America as about a determined examination of its own essential qualities. Neither is the dialectic of continuity and renewal unique to Ireland. Wherever the insistent tempo of modernization is felt, the need for an enduring sense of identity is felt too.

Looking back, it is clear that in their work over the past twenty years— through their attitude to context, function, form, and construction—O'Donnell + Tuomey have consistently addressed issues of social change and cultural identity in Ireland. Beyond its architectural quality, it is this sense of broader cultural purpose that gives the work its depth. And yet, if Irish culture is central to this architecture, the corollary is true only in a more limited sense. For while it is evident that contemporary architecture has become far more prominent in the nation's self-image and that, particularly within cities, the presence of good new buildings is now a source of pride rather than suspicion, the uncomfortable fact remains that Ireland's built environment continues to be dominated by the banal, the unconsidered, and the ill-conceived. The profession remains marginal to the large-scale provision of housing, workplaces, and infrastructure—the stuff of people's daily lives. Despite its evident potency, good architecture is still largely confined to fairly limited tasks at a limited scale. And while in some sense it has been precisely by limiting its focus that Irish architecture has achieved its recent success, the challenge in the coming years will be to operate at a simultaneously more ambitious and more quotidian level in order to make modern architecture truly integral to Ireland's culture.

Of course, assessing the importance of architecture to the culture depends to a large extent on how culture itself is defined, and that has proved a notoriously tricky undertaking. In his 1948 essay *Notes towards the Definition of Culture*, T. S. Eliot argued that culture constituted all that was elevating and improving in society: "Culture may even be described simply as that which makes life worth living."[9] But at the same time he understood that culture was also "the *whole way of life* of a people, from birth to grave, from morning to night and even in sleep."[10] Architecture is at its most potent when it manages to satisfy both versions of culture, when it can occupy both the high ground and the background.

In O'Donnell + Tuomey's work to date, the Ranelagh Multi-Denominational School (1998) stands out for the modest, clear-eyed manner in which it achieves this. The ease with which the domestic fabric of its suburban context is rewoven into a new pattern, the sureness and simplicity of the composition, and the generous clarity of the classrooms, all belie the many complexities of the site and brief. The building has the unmistakable feel of a project borne of close collaboration and intimate understanding. The life within the school, and its life within the community, seems to be the paramount concern. The predominant atmosphere is one of festive calm, within which the various encounters that form part of the school's daily round—the meeting of children with teachers, of children with each other, and with their parents and the world of the street outside—are each accorded the respect and formality they deserve. The architecture achieves all this, but it mostly stays quiet about it, and the building has quickly become an integral part of the community. Life—"the whole way of life of a people"—continues and is renewed. From here, it is not a great leap to that other Dublin schoolyard which, a century earlier, provided the setting for one of James Joyce's most resounding affirmations of the everyday:

The ways of the creator are not our ways, Mr. Deasy said. All history moves towards one great goal, the manifestation of God.

Stephen jerked his thumb towards the window, saying:

That is God.

Hooray! Ay! Whrrwhee!

What? Mr. Deasy asked.

A shout in the street, Stephen answered, shrugging his shoulders.[11]

[1] John Tuomey, *Architecture, Craft and Culture—Reflections on the Work of O'Donnell and Tuomey* (Cork: Gandon Editions, 2004), 30.

[2] Clifford Geertz, "After the Revolution: The Fate of Nationalism in the New States" in *The Interpretation of Cultures* (New York: Basic Books, 1973), 234.

[3] For a discussion of the interplay on essentialism and epochalism in the architecture in the new state, see for instance Hugh Campbell, "Irish Identity and the Architecture of the New State" in John Olley, Wilfred Wang and Annette Becker, eds, *Ireland: 20th Century Architecture* (Munich, New York: Prestel Verlag, 1997), 82–88.

[4] From Paul Ricoeur, "Universal Civilisation and National Cultures," [1961] quoted in Kenneth Frampton, *Modern Architecture: A Critical History* (London: Thames and Hudson, 1988), 313. Included as a chapter in the revised edition of *Modern Architecture*, the essay on critical regionalism first appeared as "Towards a Critical Regionalism: Six Points for an Architecture of Resistance" in Hal Foster, ed., *The Anti-Aesthetic: Essays on Post-Modern Culture* (Port Townsend, Washington: Bay Press, 1983), 16–30.

[5] Tuomey, *Architecture, Craft and Culture*, 30.

[6] Group 91 was a group of young architectural practices that came together specifically to enter the Temple Bar competition, although many had been involved in earlier collaborations on counterprojects, competitions, and theoretical projects for Dublin's urban development. The other members were Shay Cleary, Grafton Architects, Paul Keogh, McCullough Mulvin, McGarry NiEanaigh, Shane O'Toole, and Derek Tynan. For many of these architects, the Temple Bar project represented the culmination of a long engagement with the revitalization of the city. Most went on to build individual projects in the area.

[7] Niall McCullough and Valerie Mulvin, *A Lost Tradition: The Nature of Architecture in Ireland* (Cork: Gandon Editions, 1987).

[8] Profile of Philip Roth, *Guardian*, 12 July 2004.

[9] T. S. Eliot, *Notes Towards a Definition of Culture* (London: Faber and Faber, 1948), 27.

[10] Eliot, *Notes*, 31. Eliot's work is among the many critiques of culture analyzed in Terry Eagleton, *The Idea of Culture* (Oxford: Blackwell, 2000).

[11] James Joyce, *Ulysses* [1922] (Oxford: Oxford University Press, 1993), 34.

Irish Pavilion

Irish Museum of Modern Art, Dublin, 1991

The Irish Pavilion was our first public building. Designed to represent Ireland at the 11 Cities/11 Nations exhibition in Leeuwarden, the Netherlands, the small, temporary structure was a collaboration with the Irish artist Brian Maguire. Despite its temporary character, it was built three times: first in a warehouse in Dublin, then in the exhibition hangar in Leeuwarden, and finally for the inauguration of the Irish Museum of Modern Art in the summer of 1991.

Made of timber and corrugated iron, the little red shed stood for six weeks like a Trojan horse in the gravel courtyard of the converted military hospital. Using elements such as ladders and catwalks we created a contemplative space that was intended to intensify the experience of viewing each of the twelve exhibited paintings by Maguire. Part house, part studio, and evoking both prison and gallery associations, the pavilion echoed Maguire's reluctantly lyrical paintings of isolation and loss.

The structure was the first object that visitors encountered in the first room of the new museum, where it was regarded with suspicion and disdain by most of the press, some of the public, and a few of our friends. However, soon after it was dismantled for scrap, people began to lament its absence, complaining that the courtyard was not the same without it. This experience taught us a lesson about the emotional reach of expressive architectural form, and we moved on from that moment to further explore the complicated territory of character and identity. To paraphrase Peter Smithson, our intention was not just to build but to communicate.

Opening of the Irish Museum of Modern Art

Development sketch

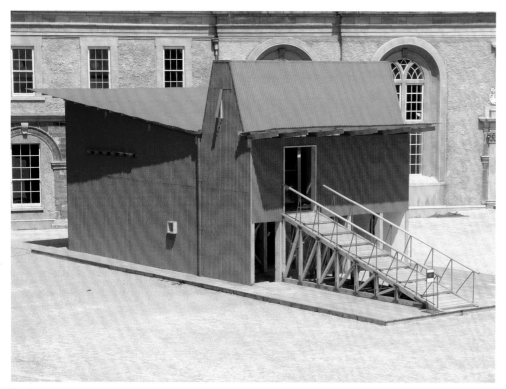

Exterior view

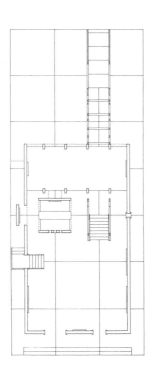

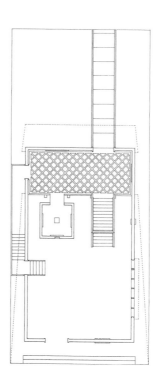

Lower floor plan

Upper floor plan

Planimetric

Doorway

Interior view toward the ramp

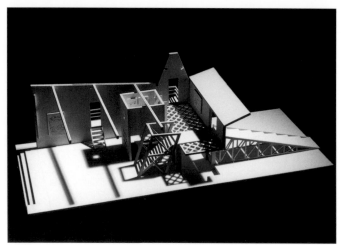

Model of interior

Ground floor with *Hanging Man*

View of upper cell

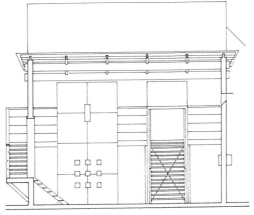

Section

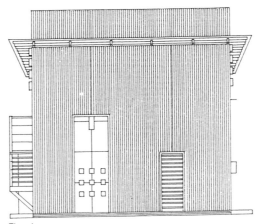

Elevation

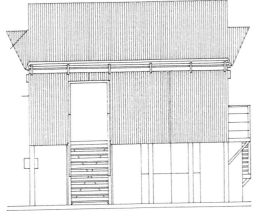

Elevation

Undercroft with prisoner portrait

Big House

Stair to cliff walk

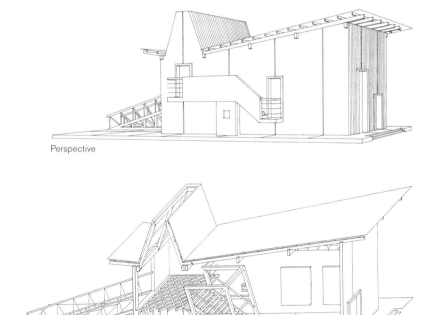

Perspective

Sectional axonometric

29

View of pavilion at dusk

Three Buildings in Temple Bar

Dublin

Irish Film Centre, 1992
National Photographic Archive, 1996
Gallery of Photography, 1996

We spent ten years working on one block in Temple Bar, Dublin's cultural quarter. We started on the conversion of the former Quaker Meeting House into the Irish Film Centre in 1986, and Meeting House Square, with the National Photographic Archive and the Gallery of Photography, was opened to the public in 1996.

The Quakers had accumulated a cluster of overlapping properties, which they built up around the seventeenth-century foundations of their mid-block meeting house. Our site-specific strategy for the new film center—comprising new interventions, surgical demolitions, simple conversion, and invisible mending—was intended to continue the process of gradual change and incremental adaptation that had characterized the historical development of this complex site.

The opportunity for new building was limited to the edges, with an opened-up courtyard forming the heart of the project. Four pedestrian routes from surrounding streets connect to the glass-roofed foyer, which, by its stone and steel floor, pigmented rendered surfaces, and lines of neon lighting, integrates the new cinema uses with the old urban fabric. The building cluster accommodates various aspects of film culture, including two movie theaters, a film archive, bookshop, restaurant, bar, education rooms, and film production offices.

Our design did not propose to contrast new with old, nor was it divided between historical conservation and contemporary design interventions. Rather, our intention was to make a case study of the co-dependent interaction of layers of time in the living present. Working slowly on this project, through the processes of research, survey, design, demolition, repair, re-use, building, and re-building, set us on a course by which we still steer today—the belief that the task of architecture is continuity and renewal.

While the Irish Film Centre was under construction, we worked together with a group of friends and colleagues, Group 91, on a cooperative competition entry for the Framework Development Plan for Temple Bar. This area of Dublin had been scheduled for demolition and comprehensive redevelopment, and the competition brief set out an alternative proposition for its regeneration as a cultural quarter. In some ways the design of the film center as a "cultural cluster" served as a pilot project for the larger-scale urban development strategy. The projects proposed in the development plan, which was based on the consolidation of the existing character and the conservation of the urban fabric, included the National Photographic Archive and the Gallery of Photography on Meeting House Square.

Their pivotal location in Temple Bar suggested the need for both buildings to have a strong presence. The archive is a heavy structure packed with dark spaces for the conservation, storage, and exhibition of 250,000 light-sensitive glass plate negatives. Lecture rooms and studio spaces sit on top of the structural arch. The requirement to exclude daylight led to the heavily modeled facade, while the brickwork relates to the material quality of Dublin's buildings.

The gallery, which includes exhibition space, darkrooms, and a bookstore, is a north-facing building of white stone, with a large window in the front facade as its central organizing element. Hinged and sliding screens in the gallery spaces can be positioned to double the available wall-hanging space for larger exhibitions, making the rooms flexible for a varied program of changing exhibitions. The large-scale "shutter-lens" window mechanism operates as a screen for films and photographs that are projected from the National Photographic Archive across the square. The two buildings are joined by a beam of light projected from a metal box in the archive to the window screen of the gallery.

The outdoor projections, which were inspired by *Cinema Paradiso* and by outdoor movie screenings we had seen in Venice and Barcelona, have become a regular part of summer nights in Temple Bar. Watching *The Birds* in the open air with seagulls wheeling overhead adds to the scary drama of Hitchcock's scenario.

Irish Film Centre, 1992

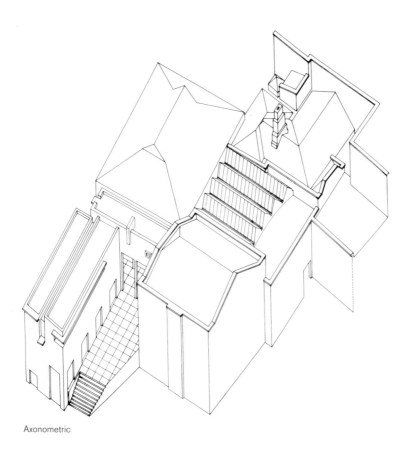

Axonometric

Elevation to Sycamore Street showing urban context
before Temple Bar redevelopment, 1992

The Quaker Meeting House's covered yard
before work started on site

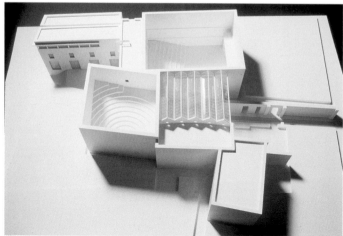

Model

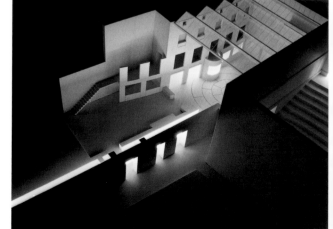

Light study model

View of foyer in daylight

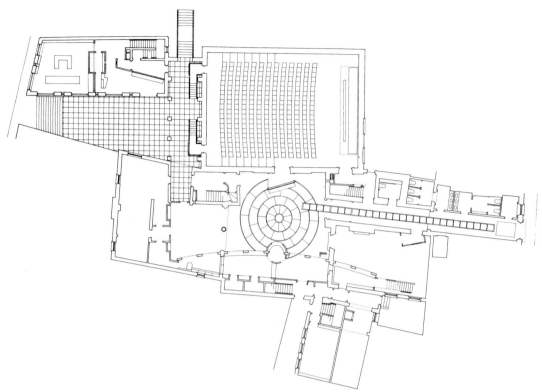

Ground floor plan

The roof-lit foyer

National Photographic Archive, 1996

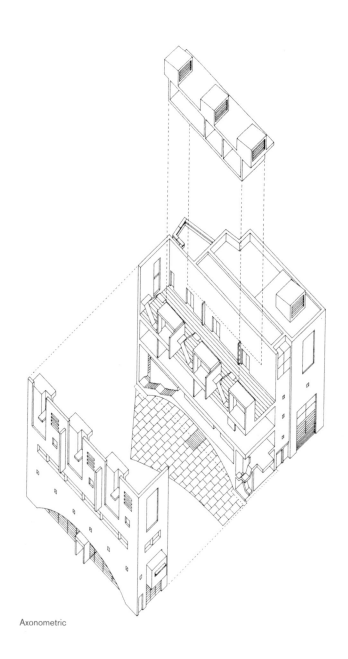

Axonometric

Elevation to Meeting House Square

Projection box

The building is a bridge between street and square.

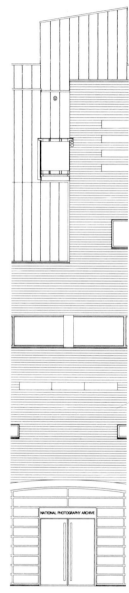

Elevation detail

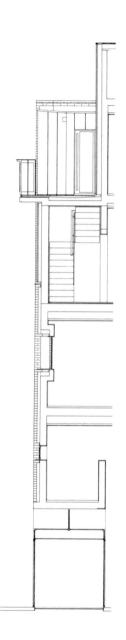

Steel counter, stone floor

Gallery of Photography, 1996

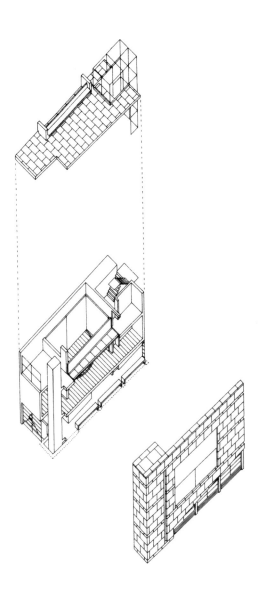

Axonometric

North Elevation

Model

Stair to roof terrace

The gallery on the square

Window to the square

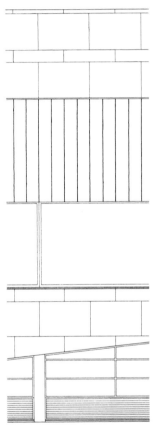

Elevation detail

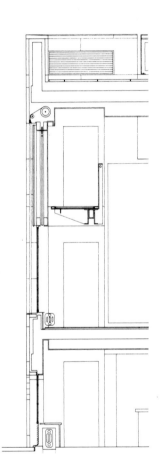

Gallery space with exhibition

Aerial view of Temple Bar

The Birds screening on Meeting House Square

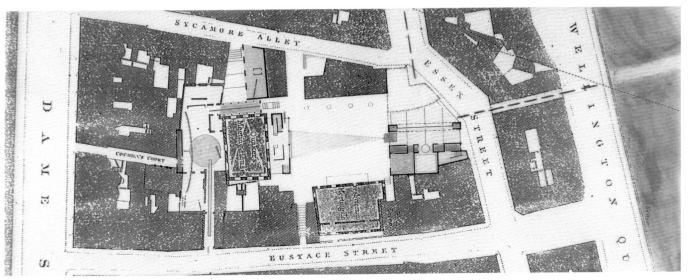

Three projects in Temple Bar on 1847 ordnance survey map of Dublin

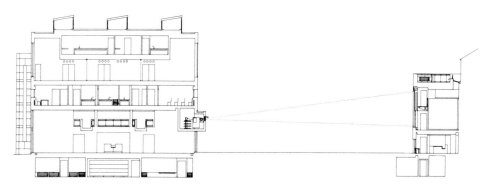

Section showing path of projection

Inaugural film showing on Meeting House Square, June 1996

Blackwood Golf Centre

Clandeboye, County Down, Northern Ireland, 1994

Our design for a new kind of golf club in the pastoral demesne of Clandeboye House
was a tribute to our mentor, Jim Stirling, who died on the day we started drawing up
the scheme. The competition brief emphasized the social and environmental aspirations
of the project, which was envisioned as an open, welcoming facility in a protected
landscape. Our response was to disaggregate the various parts of the clubhouse program
and to regroup disparate elements, each one specific to its purpose, on a built-up
embankment. Like Stirling's Leicester Building lying on its side, this cluster of different
structures is held together by a long organizing line. The curved driving range is cut into
a raised courtyard overlooking the landscape.

While neither of us had ever thought about playing golf, we were frustrated by
the hermetically sealed introversion of any clubhouse we had seen. The idea of external
circulation between the changing rooms, bar, and shop seemed a more appropriate
response to the outdoor nature of the game. Eventually, and by gradual degrees, the
building was taken over by a high-class restaurant.

View from ninth tee

Window box

Reception room with window boxes and south-facing roof light

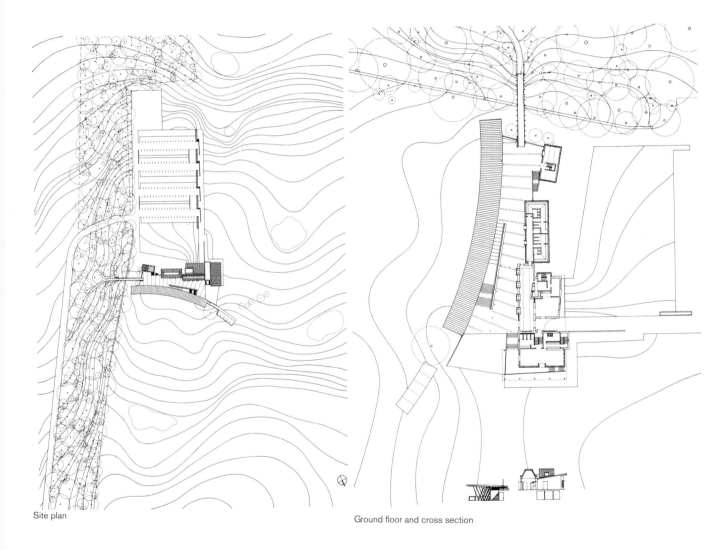

Site plan

Ground floor and cross section

Driving range and courtyard

Courtyard

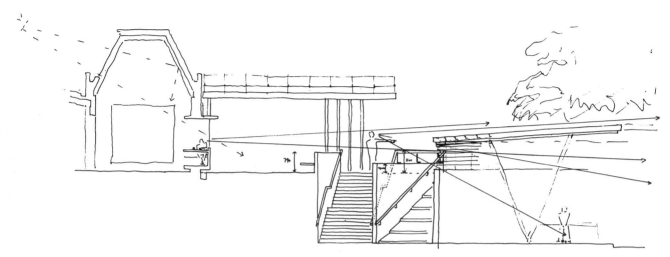

Sketch section explaining relationship between built elements and land

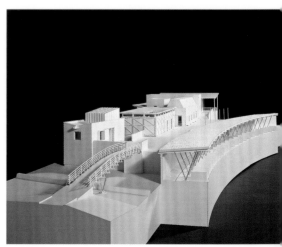

Model

Golfers on the eighteenth hole

Hudson House

Navan, County Meath, Ireland, 1998

The scheme for this small family house was devised from the peculiar conditions of the site. The plan is organized around a central sunken courtyard, the footprint of a disused workshop in the back garden of an ordinary two-story terraced house. One-story-height retaining walls hold back the higher-level neighboring gardens on either side of the court, while the house itself is designed as a two-part building. A living space and a bedroom tower are positioned at either end of the yard, with external circulation between the living and sleeping zones. The cast-in-situ cranked roof gives the living space a cave-like character, so that the concepts of cave, courtyard, and tower become the main elements of this excavated house. The only entrance to the complex is off a tiny courtyard accessed through an archway from the street.

The project was realized in three stages, due to separately organized contracts: excavation and drainage; concrete structural shell; and carpentry/joinery completions. Given the lack of connection between the building trades, this process imposed a certain rigor on the design. Each stage of the work was approached as an overlay on the preceding phase of construction. We were reminded of the economy of means of medieval tower houses with their clear delineation between the methods of masons and carpenters, and between structure and fabric. The experience of this small building informed our strategy for subsequent larger-scale projects such as the separation of concrete ground works from timber superstructure in Letterfrack and the separate parts held together by a common courtyard in the Glucksman Gallery.

Site with sunken ruined workshop

Pencil planimetric

Courtyard-facade relationship

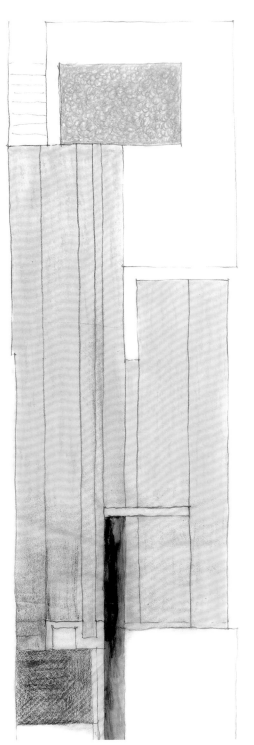

Stone floor lines

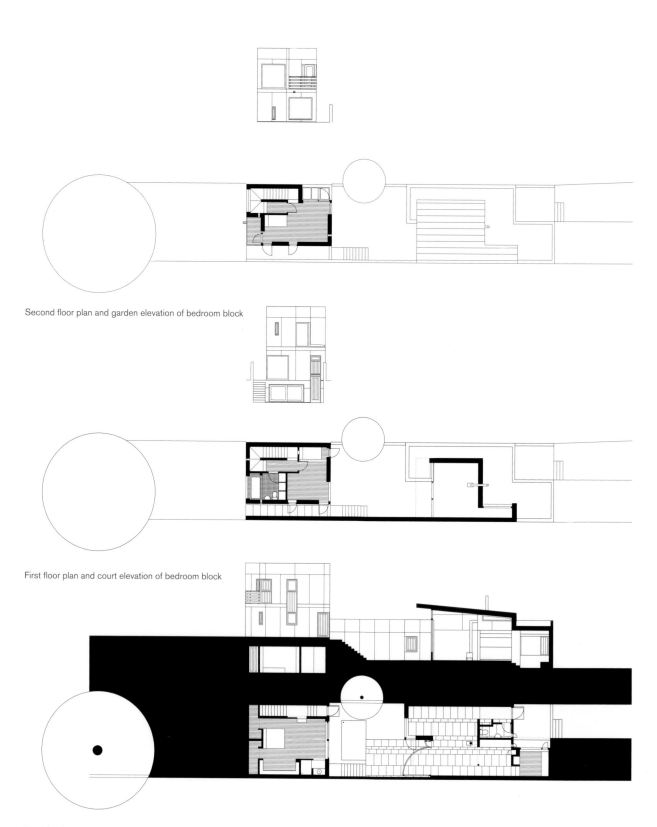

Second floor plan and garden elevation of bedroom block

First floor plan and court elevation of bedroom block

Combined ground floor plan and section

Site study model

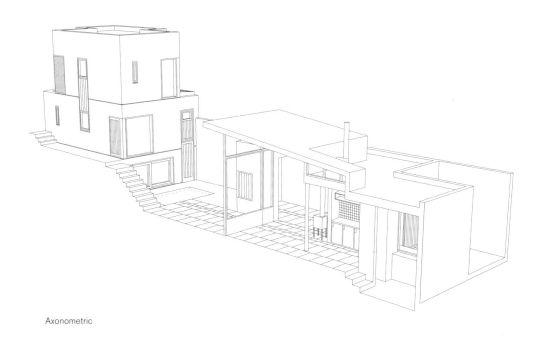

Design model

Axonometric

Bedroom tower

Concrete shell under construction

A glazed screen door connects the living and courtyard spaces.

Cave, courtyard, and tower

Clerestory light in the living room

The cavelike living room is sunken between the neighbours' gardens.

Ranelagh Multidenominational School

Ranelagh, Dublin 6, 1998

A school building can be understood as both a large house and a small town, being domestic and civic in equal measure. This eight-classroom primary school is a community building that is appropriated as a village hall in the evenings and whose yard serves as the location of the farmer's market on Sunday afternoons. Designed in careful consultation with residents and conservation groups, the school is a response to an analysis of its context, a site near the Georgian Mountpleasant Square and the houses of Ranelagh.

The new building responds to the existing street scale by breaking into multiple brick elements on the front facade, while its rhythmic volumes are unified at the back under a long cantilevered wooden canopy. The expression of the interlocking internal and external spaces, which function as playgrounds, classrooms, and an assembly hall, is plain, with a clear order. The materials, brick and wood, were chosen for their hard weathering qualities, so the new building would be quickly assimilated as a permanent presence into the everyday urban background.

Four brick houses face the street.

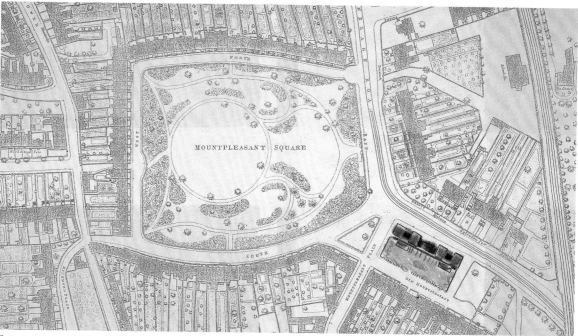
Concept sketch on 1847 ordnance survey map of Dublin

The playground is on the south.

The roof terrace is an outdoor teaching space.

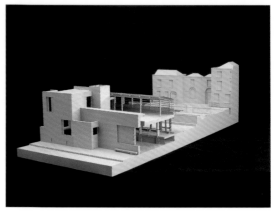

Design model

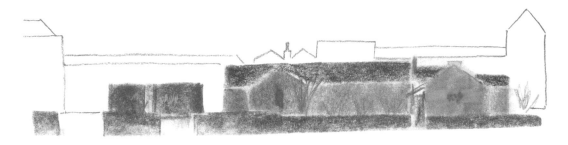

existing massing to Ranelagh Road

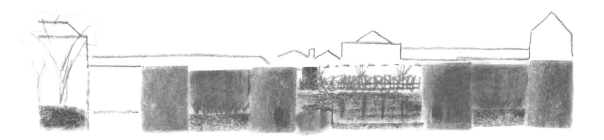

proposed massing to Ranelagh Road

Development of elevations: sketches of existing and proposed schemes

A snowy day

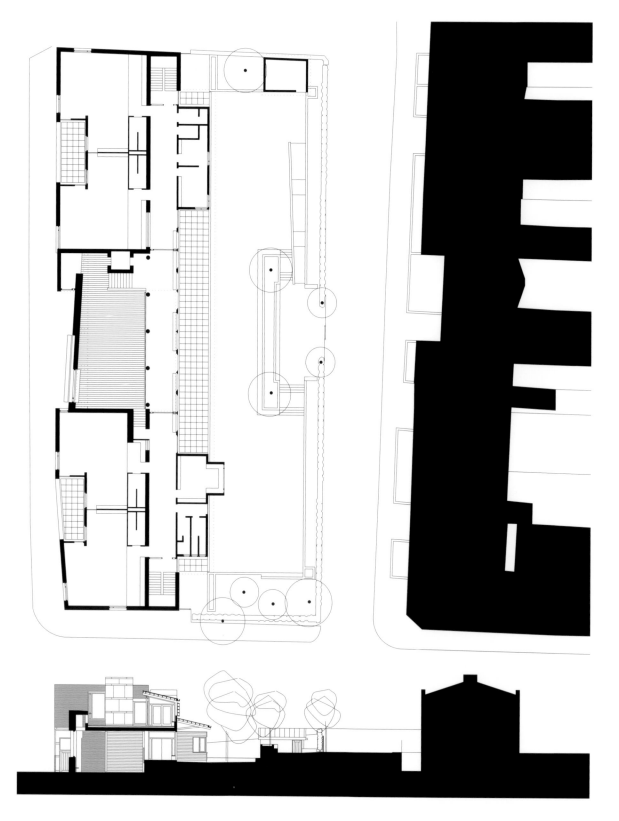

Combined ground floor plan and section

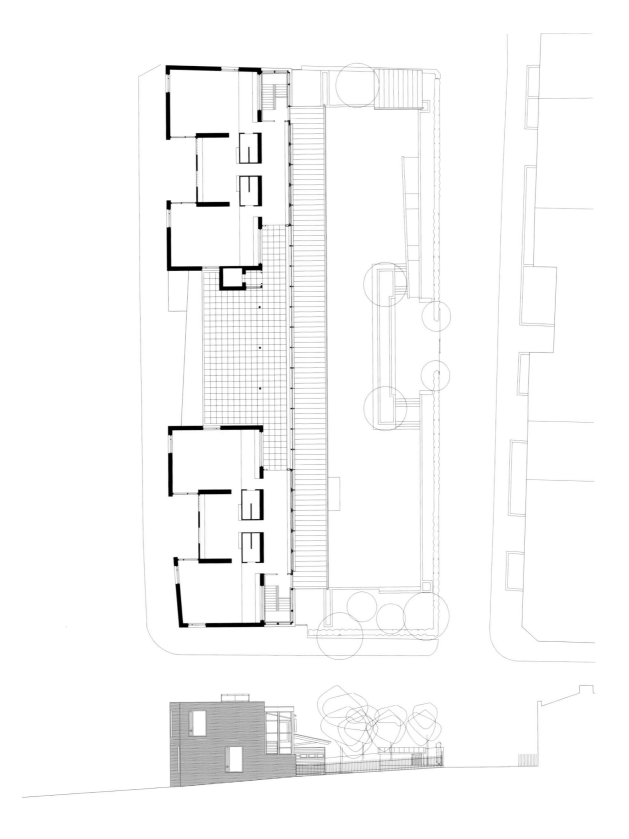

Combined first floor plan and northwest elevation

Classroom courtyard

Wide corridor

Salvaged bricks make up the north wall of the school facing busy Ranelagh Road.

Furniture College Letterfrack

Letterfrack, County Galway, Ireland, 2001

What now seems to us a sublimely scenic landscape must once have presented a bleak and disorienting prospect to the inmates of this former reform school for boys from the city slums. Built as an alternative to the desperate social conditions of the late-nineteenth century, the industrial schools degenerated into institutions where cruelty and harshness were widespread. After the retreat of the religious orders in the 1970s, the redundant structure was acquired by Connemara West, a community development group that was looking for an antidote to the cycle of rural depopulation and encroaching tourism. A woodwork skills training project gave rise to a thriving Furniture College program. We were asked to prepare a campus plan that would allow the college to develop into the twenty-first century, including the design of new structures and the refurbishment of the former industrial school. We realized that within the explicit brief for future planning and functional building lay a deeper implicit requirement for transformation—to banish the ghosts and, by opening up the closed institution, to renew the ground.

The history of the site provided a basis for our scheme. We were interested in the strategy of cut-and-fill that grounds the older buildings into the hillside but at the same time we were determined to transform the institutional self-containment of the former industrial school. We decided to keep the sound structural shell of the old building, but to loosen its bonds by shifting the symmetry, clearing out the corridors, and lowering the windows to allow people to see out. The axial approach was changed into a curved line in the landscape, and a new entry forecourt opens up the closed form of the courtyard plan like a folded-out chain of different forms.

With the institutional axis extinguished, the whole scheme now hinges around a freestanding chimney, placed in the same alignment and height as the chimneys of the existing building. It fixes the forecourt and suggests a new center, which is in balanced equilibrium rather than strict symmetry. Different building structures relate to the site conditions of inconsistent rock and boggy ground. Structural timber frames make the furniture workshops feel like places where joinery details should matter. The sawtooth roof of the bench room provides a clear-span, top-lit studio space, while the library is raised like a box of books over concrete piers that open the café out to the garden. The exercise yard of the former institution will be changed into an academic garden and will function as the social center of the furniture college.

External materials relate to the colors and textures of the landscape: Irish green oak, terned stainless steel, concrete, and sand-pigmented render are designed to weather naturally and to register the passage of time.

Landscape near Connemara West

Students at the former reform school for boys

The Furniture College Letterfrack is nestled in the mountains.

Roof forms in the landscape

Concept sketch

New and old buildings seen from the west

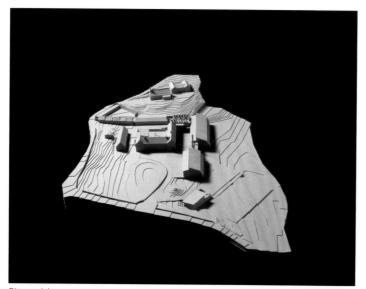

Site model

South elevation

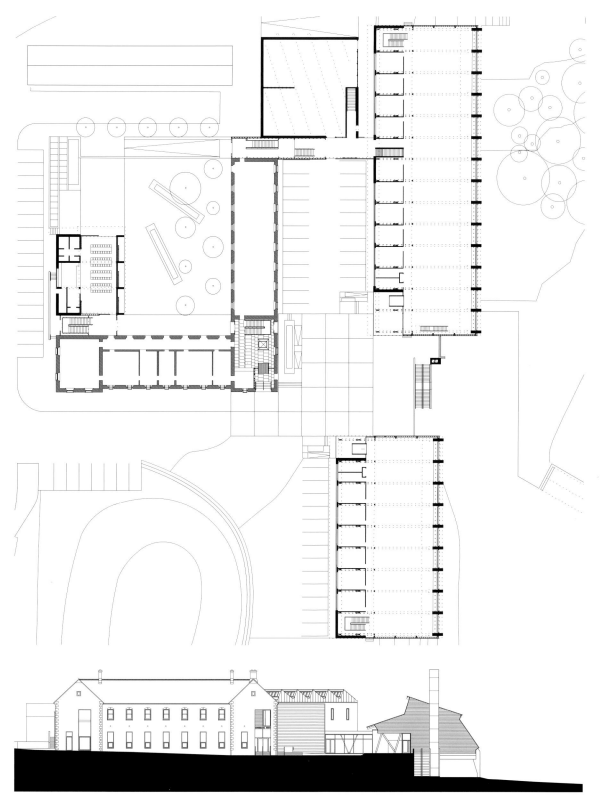

Combined ground floor plan and south elevation

Library windows

Library over café

Entry porches

Academic garden

Entry forecourt

The machine hall gables are clad with green oak and the timber structure is exposed at the entry.

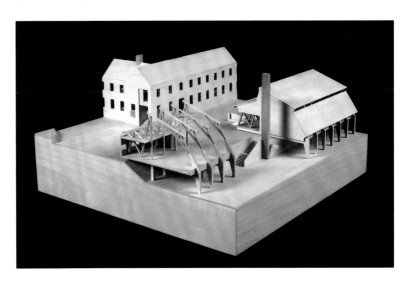

Model showing the machine hall and furniture restoration unit

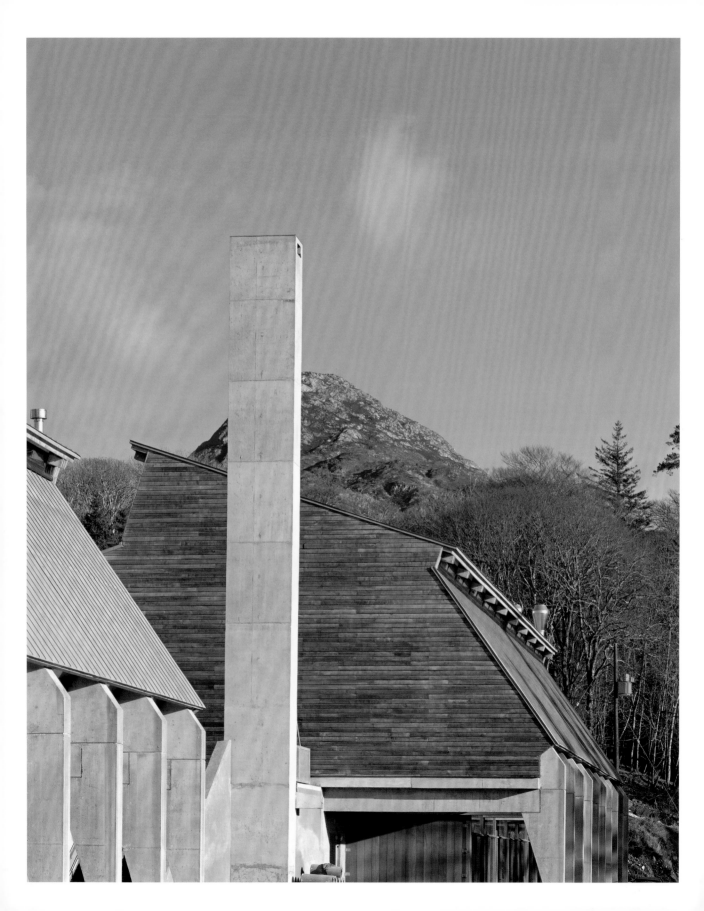

Structural timber frames in the furniture workshops

The machine hall timber frame

Café interior

The café opens out to the as yet unfinished academic garden

Mountains near Connemara West

Local beach stones

Plywood wall cladding and steel railings in library

Library window, framing the mountains

Social Housing in Galbally

Galbally, County Limerick, Ireland, 2002

Galbally is a nineteenth-century planned village, laid out around a square at the crossroads in the dairy pastureland of County Limerick. Sadly, council housing estates often appear extraneous to any existing settlement pattern. Our objective here was to treat this small social housing scheme—six three-story family houses and five single-story houses designed for old people—as an extension of the village. In the Irish vernacular tradition, plain plastered terraces of houses line the approaches to country market towns such as Galbally, a development pattern known as *sráid-bhaile*, or "street-town." Given the sloping ground conditions, we chose to tilt the two pitched rooflines counter to one another and to step their porch thresholds with the contour of the site. Each house, rendered in traditional materials, is painted with its own pair of colors, giving it identity in the complex. The porches are provided with the social focus of a built-in terrazzo bench and planting box, an in-between social zone between house and town.

Three-story family houses with mid-level living spaces and gardens

Earth-colored porch reveals identify each house within the terrace.

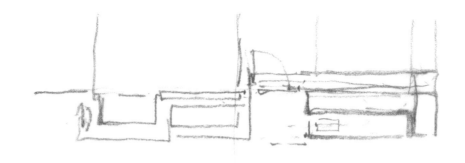

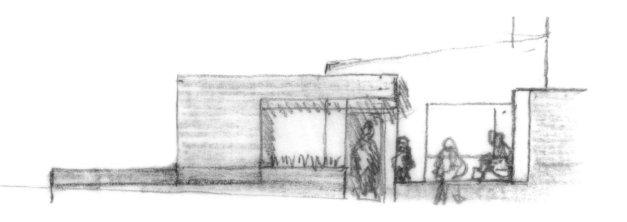

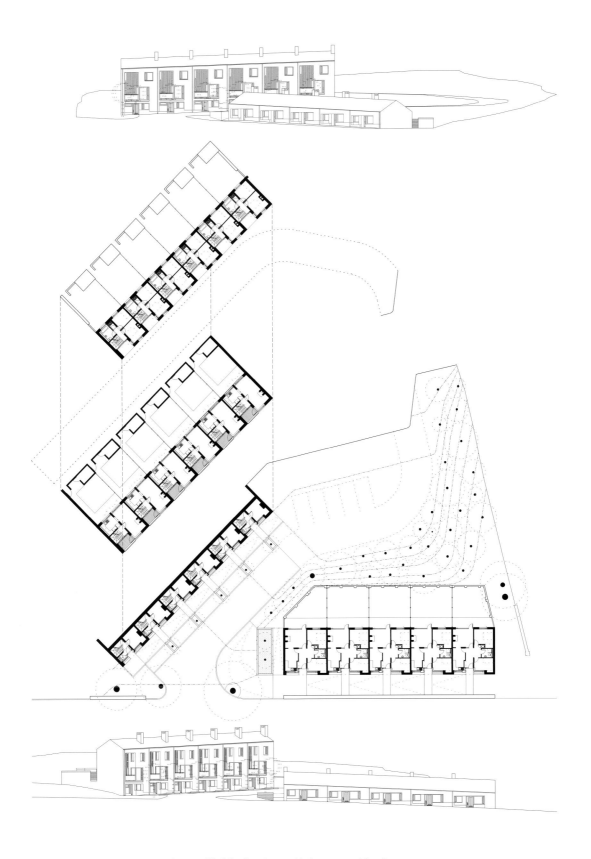

Each house steps up from the next; the overall building line slopes with the contour of the site.

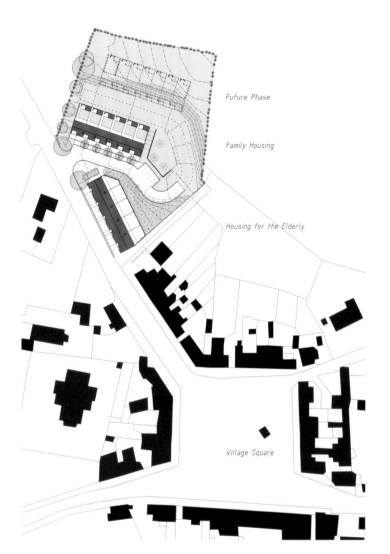

Future Phase

Family Housing

Housing for the Elderly

Village Square

Terraced houses extend the pattern of the nineteenth-century planned village.

Model

Houses for the elderly on the village street

Terrazzo seat, planting box, and threshold define
a social zone between house and village.

Leinster House Press Reception Room

Leinster House, Dublin, 2002

This transformation of an existing stairhall in a landlocked corner of the Irish Parliament buildings into a small stone amphitheater was a minor public project. Busloads of schoolchildren, brought by their teachers on tours of the Dáil, assemble in this room to meet their local parliamentary representatives. Its function as a press reception room is served by a television interview studio that is tucked into the undercroft of the raked seating.

The existing stairhall, a cube of approximately twenty-seven feet, with a central oval skylight and a single Georgian door to a covered arcade in the forecourt of Leinster House, had become a left-over space between recent rebuilding works for parliamentary offices and the National Library. We tried to make something more permanent out of what was initially envisaged as a simple conversion and technical outfitting of the existing eighteenth-century hallway. A fragmentary amphitheater was carved out of portland stone and positioned slightly skewed within the existing shell. Its symmetry is distorted by the differently fixed positions of the skylight, door, lectern, and projection screen, so that the space itself appears to shift its weight, *contrapposto*, to meet the flow of schoolchildren across its terraced landscape.

The splayed seats of the oak benches focus on the lectern.

View of existing entrance door

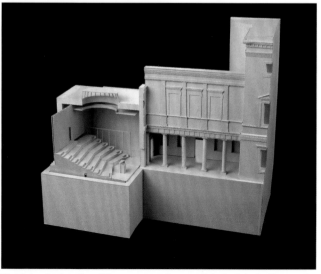

Model showing insertion of the press reception room into the Leinster House colonnade

Auditorium

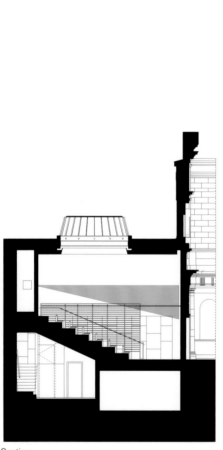

Section

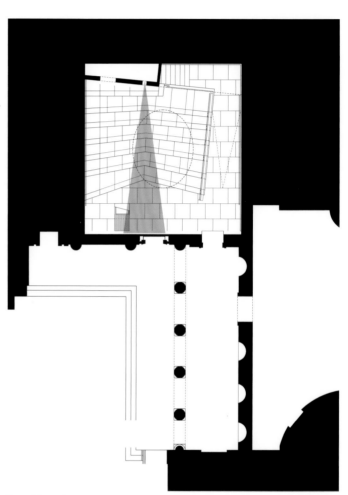

Ground floor plan

Stone steps in auditorium

Detail of stone steps and steel railing

Lyric Theatre

Belfast, Northern Ireland, designed 2003, for completion 2007

The Lyric Theatre is a new complex for the Lyric production company, consisting of a 400-seat theater and 150-seat studio space and related facilities located along the banks of the River Lagan. The winner of an international design competition, our scheme for the building centers on the auditorium: a single-rake theater and fly tower stage are contained within a crystalline form, around which different operational networks are gathered. In our design we have tried to reveal the backstage functions, allowing the various supporting activities to wrap around the foyer spaces.

In a production company such as the Lyric, everyone works closely together, from the front-of-house administrators, the actors, directors, and costume designers to the backstage technicians. The company is like a big family, and our goal was to make a house for Lyric. Overlapping functions are folded around the central auditorium, and the interdependence and interaction of the theater way of life is made more legible to the audience.

Seen from the river, the theater is a luminous, translucent presence in the surrounding parkland. On Ridgeway Street it is the last building in a line of brick structures. Built in angular Belfast brick, it will be anchored to the street, while its flowing spaces for public circulation echo the haze of the Lagan River. It is embedded, permanent, here to stay, and at the same time expresses a dynamic fluidity that is open to change.

Ramped entry forecourt

Entry foyer

View from upper foyer

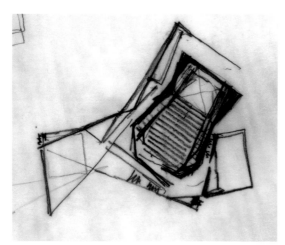

Early sketch development

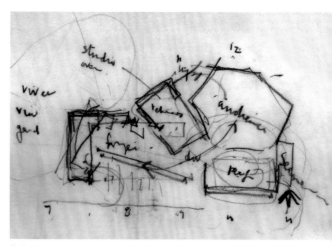

Early sketch development

Outside the rehearsal room

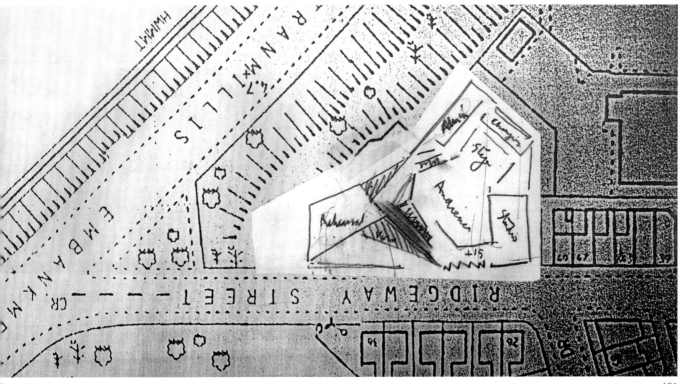

Sketch on site plan

122   Context model

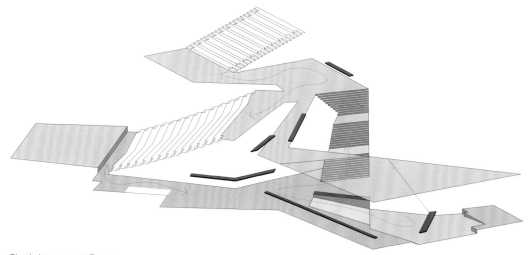

Circulation concept diagram

Auditorium study model

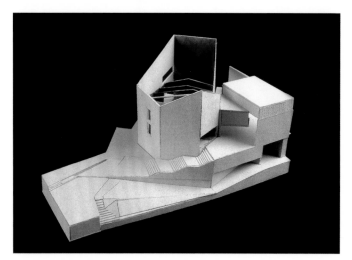

Massing study model

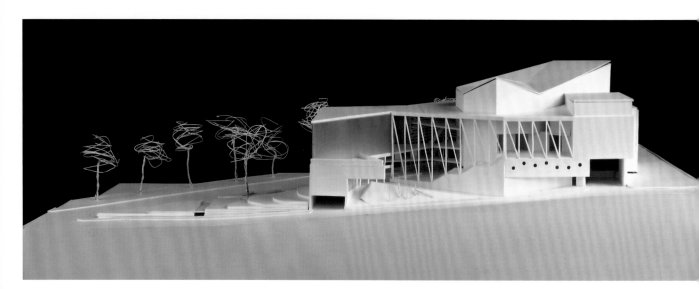

Model showing Ridgeway Street elevation

Promenade / staging possibilities

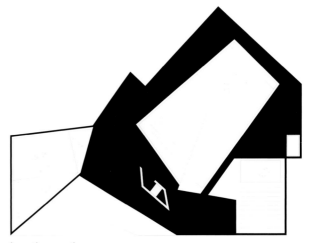

Acoustic separation zones

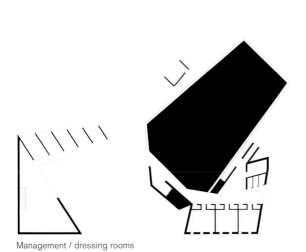

Management / dressing rooms

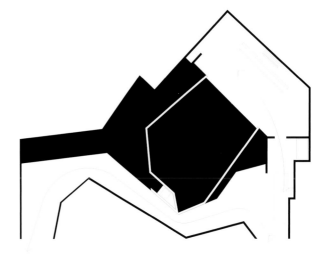

Backstage access

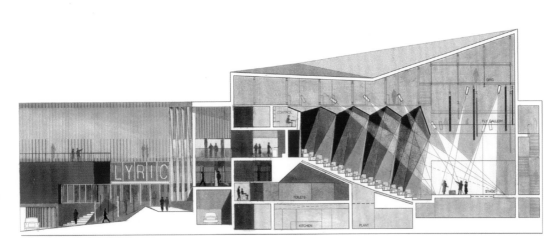

Long section through theatre

River elevation

Opening night at the Lyric

Medical Research Laboratories

University College Dublin, 2003

Sited near the gates of the suburban campus of University College Dublin, this building, the outcome of an architectural competition, comprises two distinct functions: the single-story extension of an existing routine testing facility, the Virus Reference Laboratory; and the provision of new laboratories for highly specialized research into exotic diseases. Our scheme gathered the testing laboratories around an internal landscaped courtyard and placed the research laboratories on stilts to face northwards out to sea, resembling artist's studios designed for scientists in creative concentration.

Offices and research laboratories face each other across a central stairhall that provides space for social interaction. The structure of the building is designed to allow for flexibility of layout and equipment to provide for the changing technical specifications of laboratory requirements.

For reasons of limited funding, and given the fixed cost of laboratory equipment, the building had to be cheaply constructed in lightweight dry construction. We wrapped the steel frame in fiber cement panels, with timber-clad conference facilities sheltered underneath the main body of the building. All fumes are filtered and funneled through the roof chimney formation. The building, in use night and day, becomes a beacon of university research work.

Extract fumes are filtered and exhausted through the high chimney roof form.

View from campus entrance

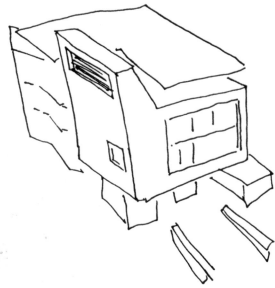

Development sketch

Research laboratories are raised above the library.

North elevation

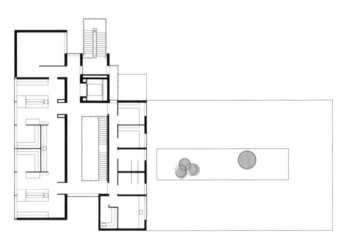

First floor plan

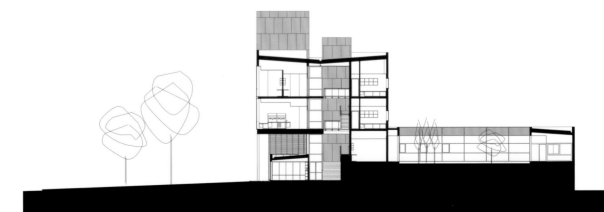

Section

The building overlooks the campus landscape.

North-facing laboratories provide maximum daylight with minimum solar gain

Model

Timber-clad library in the undercroft of the laboratory

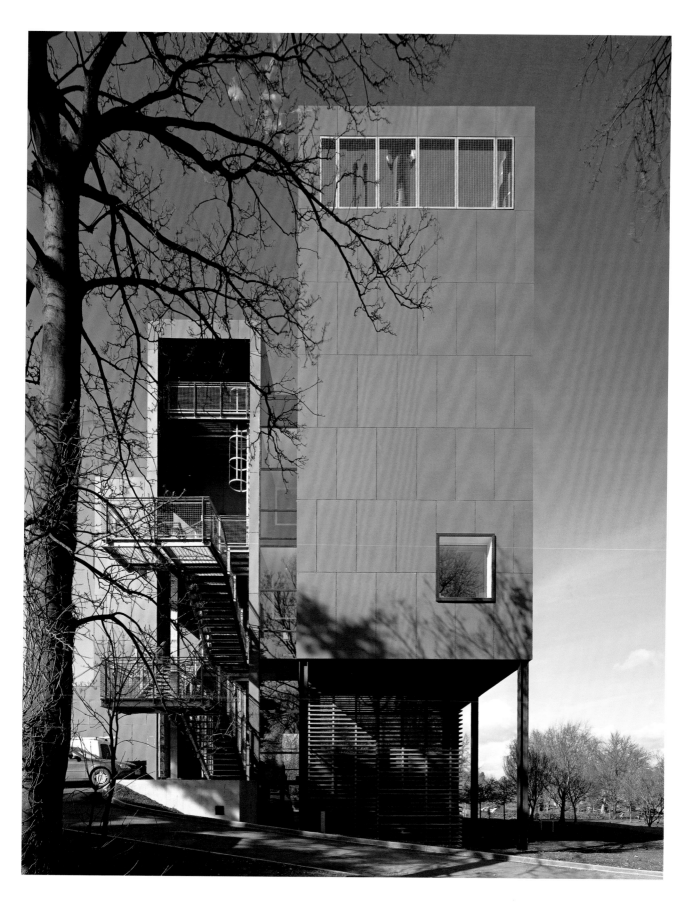

Howth House

Howth, County Dublin, 2003

This house, situated on the slope of the hill of Howth, is designed to look out at the sea. Flanked by existing houses on either side, it faces north, with a panoramic view to the island of Ireland's Eye and Howth harbor. The clients had been living next door in a Victorian villa, a house of many rooms; they wanted a convivial living space, which more loosely accommodated contemporary family life. The shape of the house is extended like a telescope. It is designed as a device for directing light through from the south and views out to the north, but its scale is determined by everyday domestic routines. The dimensions relate to the fixed points of fireplace and kitchen, with the dining table as the center around which the plan revolves.

The three-story stepped section is notched out of the sloping ground of the site. Long, load-bearing walls bend to cup the space and frame the view. No columns or cross-walls interrupt the flowing space, and transparency is maintained along the length of the house. The structure takes its lateral stability from concrete floor slabs. The concrete ceilings are boardmarked in correspondence with the floorboard pattern of the rooms. Timber floors turn up at their edges to make partitions and balustrades, avoiding any secondary detail of railings or skirtings.

Seeking to find the form of the house out of the various restrictions of the site conditions, we arrived at a sort of dream-image archetype: a building that sits sheltered, settled against a rock, looking out on the light change on the water.

South elevation by day

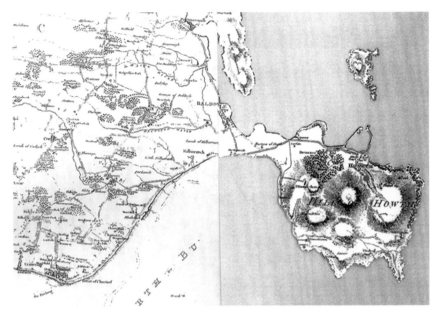

Location map

House in context

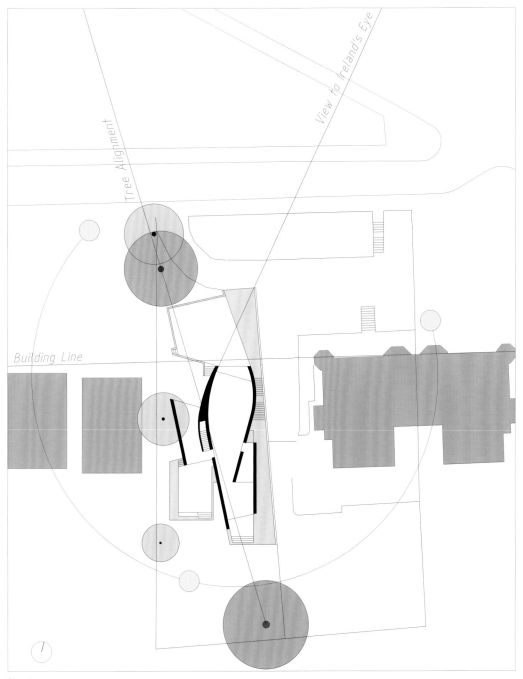

Site plan

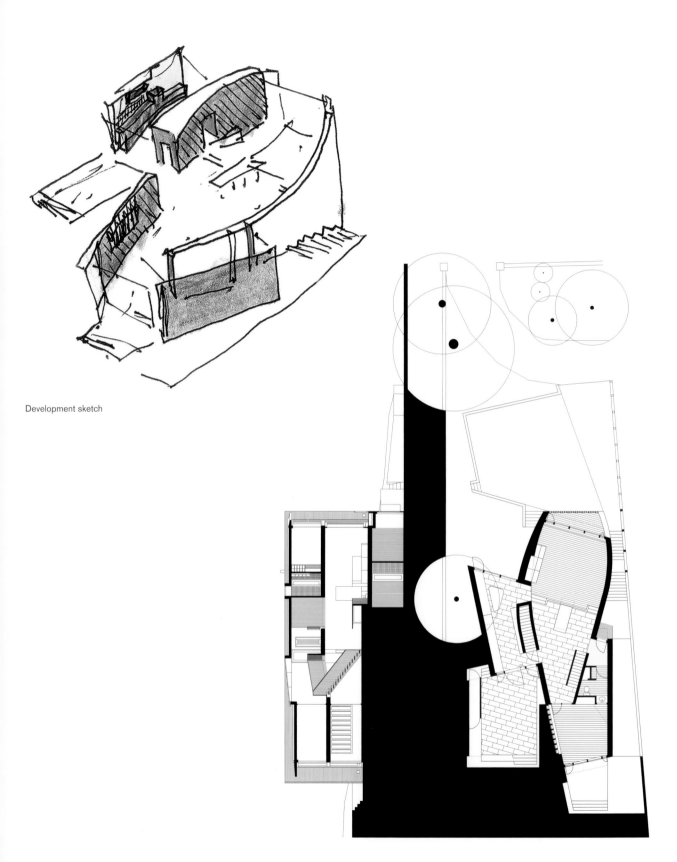

Development sketch

Combined ground floor plan and section

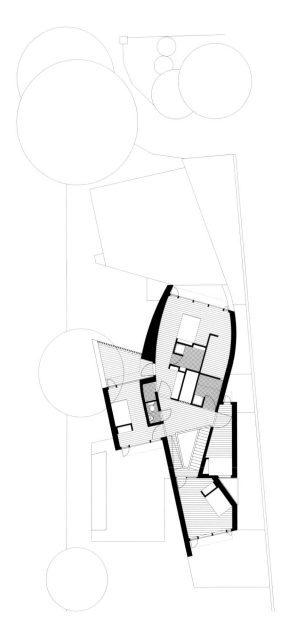

First floor plan

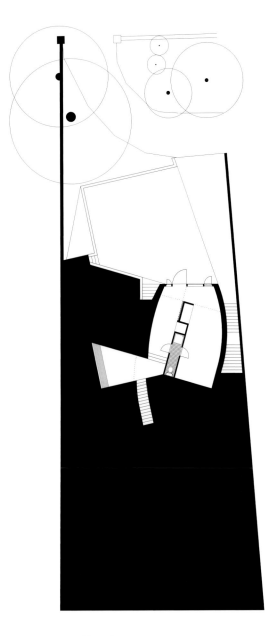

Lower ground floor plan

The walls bend to cup the space that flows between them.

The house is extended like a telescope.

Boardmarked concrete spans between walls.

The timber floors turn up at the edges to make partitions and balustrades.

Skylight in the family room

Ireland's Pavilion at the Venice Biennale

Venice, Italy, 2004

In response to the theme of the Venice Biennale 2004, "Metamorph," Ireland's Pavilion told the story of our ongoing project for the phased redevelopment of the former Industrial School in Letterfrack and its eventual incorporation within a community-generated campus: the transformation of an institution. The installation in the Arsenale displayed the past, present, and projected future of the site, focusing on the architecture of the new Furniture College while at the same time providing an overview of the history, culture, and landscape of Connemara West. The new buildings at Letterfrack represent a rethinking of the former penal institution's relationship with its place. Ireland's Pavilion recast elements of the architectural project to suggest characteristics of confinement and release, closed institutions, and frameworks for change.

Under the roof trusses of the abandoned Artiglierie munitions factory within the Arsenale, two separate structures called the Scary House and the Open Frame confronted one another in an analogous composition. Principles of form and construction, abstracted from the built reality of a contemporary college, evoked memories of island chapels, lobster pots, and the skeletal carcasses of upturned boats.

Scary House

screen

viewer

projector.

Scary House, sketch

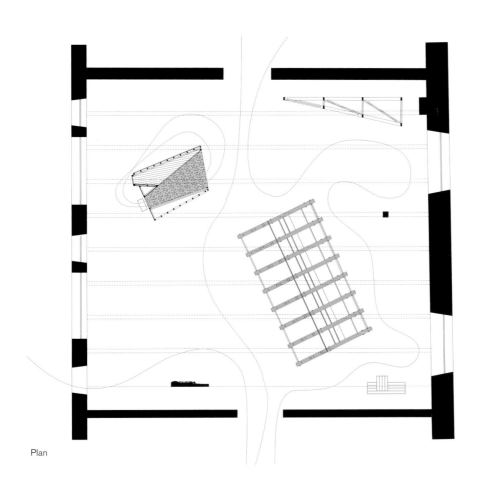

Plan

Scary House and Open Frame

Open Frame, standing panels

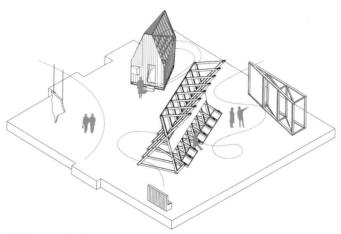

Initial concept sketch

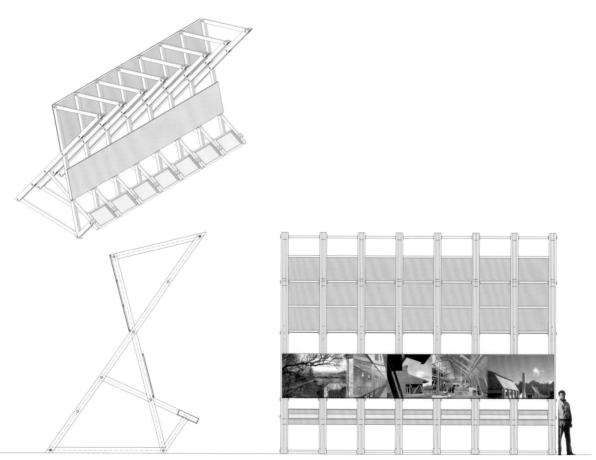

Open Frame

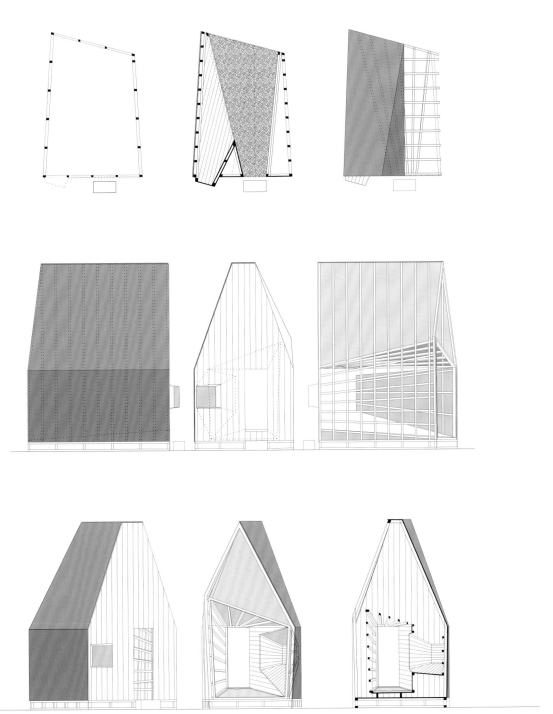

Scary House

Scary House and Open Frame

Canvas curraghs

Island chapel

Settle Bench

Sheila O'Donnell and John Tuomey on Settle Bench

Glucksman Gallery

University College Cork, 2004

The site for this new art gallery and restaurant is the Lower Ground of University College Cork, originally river-run meadowland below the cliff-top college quadrangle— an undisturbed landscape haven that formed an integral part of the picturesque setting of the protected structure of the nineteenth-century university. We intended the new building to further integrate this area into the college campus; at the same time the landscape of the Lower Grounds should be preserved. To this end we quickly established some rules for our design proposal: to stay within the footprint of two existing tennis courts; to protect existing trees; to connect the college to the river; and, by building tall between the trees, to preserve the remaining parkland.

The gallery's groundwork is a response to the geological reading of the site. We extended the limestone escarpment of the main avenue down to the riverside walk and located all service facilities, the café, and conference rooms within this plinth podium. The gallery itself is raised up like a ship in the air, with its sidewalls bending to avoid tree branches and opening out to direct views up and down the river and toward college and city landmarks. The gallery rooms provide a variety of exhibition conditions, from close control to natural daylight.

Between the overhead vessel hull and the limestone pier a new ground is opened up for the campus; a forecourt or gathering space underneath the main part of the building extends the parkland environment into the enclosed world of the gallery. While visitors are concentrating on the artworks they can pause to look into the trees, while looking at the river they can think about the exhibition—like reading a book on a train, alternating immersion and distraction can make an unconscious contribution to the conscious experience.

The café is carved out of the limestone podium.

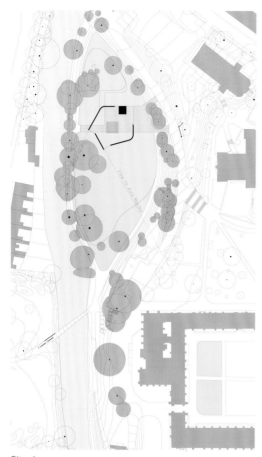

Site plan

Aerial view previous to construction

Campus parkland site

Elevation sketch

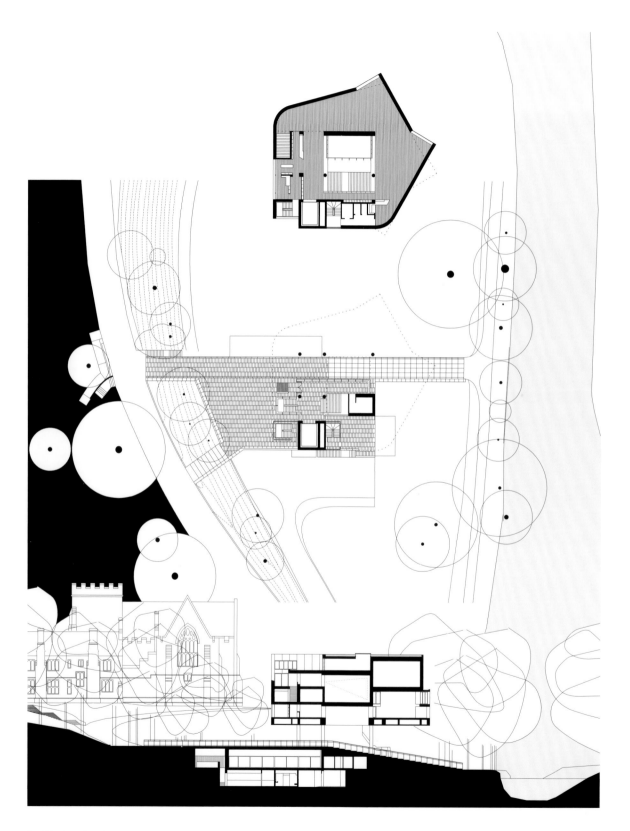

164   Combined section, first floor plan, and second floor plan

Third floor plan

Concept sketch

The gallery is raised among the trees.

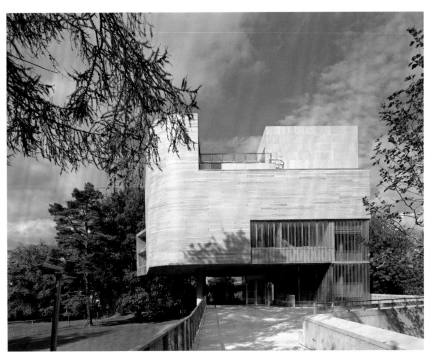

By building tall, at the height of the trees, the
building occupies a minimal footprint and the
parkland setting of the university is conserved.

Podium level entrance

 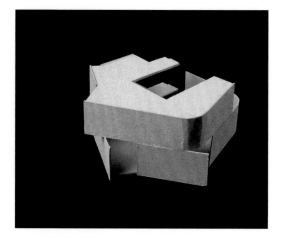

Models

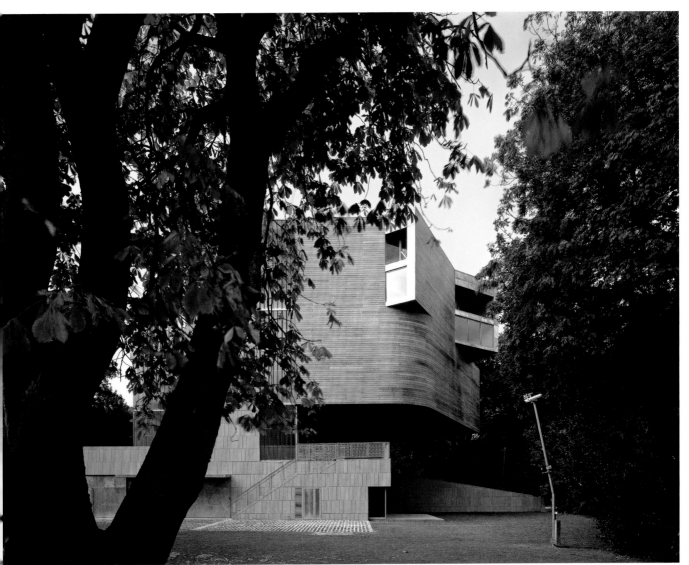

East elevation

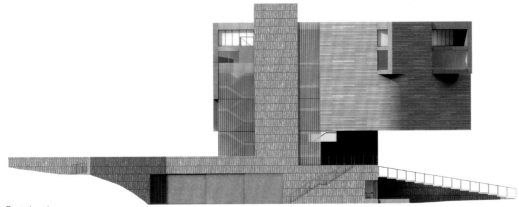

East elevation

Public route to riverside walk

Podium entry space between the timber gallery and the stone base

The undercroft entrance is an inverted courtyard between above and below.

Window detail

Gallery 1: plain white walls provide conditions for concentration, while windows control clerestory daylight and allow the mind to wander into the trees.

Gallery 1, lower level exhibition, University College Cork collection

Gallery 2, upper level exhibition, New York University collection

Undercroft

Landings and Crossings—
The Lewis Glucksman Gallery

DAVID LEATHERBARROW

"The open they came into by these moves
Stood opener, hoops came off the world,
They could feel the February air…"

—Seamus Heaney, "Crossings," from *Seeing Things*

Crossing the center of the Lewis Glucksman Gallery at the University of Cork
is a wide landing that both ends a flight of steps climbing from a river walk and
begins a ramp that slopes gently upward to meet a path heading to the heart of the
university. The prominence of this central platform is striking because landings are
normally thought of as marginal and discrete elements within buildings. Crossed in
the course of vertical circulation, they typically serve as turning or resting points in
a stairway. With continuity of movement principally in mind, most landings would
seem to differ from a stairway's many treads only in dimension—they are simply a
bit deeper than all the other steps. That they can stand for more than this, that they
can possess spatial, social, and seasonal meanings, like the "crossings" described
by Heaney in the epigraph above, is apparent when one considers landings outside
buildings, along routes built at the scale of topography, through gardens, parks, or
towns. Here landings serve as *clearings* by conferring orientation and giving the
sense that something new is about to begin. Heaney's image of "February air" can
be understood in a similar way, expressing the combined sense of unwrapping and
awakening one feels after the "hoops have come off" the world, a feeling of release
and possibility that ends the warmed seclusion of late winter. The same quality is
achieved in the central landing of the Glucksman Gallery, and elsewhere in the
building, as we will see.

Thinking more largely, not of topography but of territory, land in itself can be
viewed as a landing, flanked not by treads and risers but by lakes, rivers, or oceans,
for the shore at the edge of the town is just as much a landfall for a boat and its
crew as the stair's landing is for the person in the house. A landing then is not only
a thing but an event—to land is to take the arrival step. Heaney's view of crossings
suggests that something more than connection occurs in settings such as these.
Landings at any scale—territory, town, or building—are also the means by which
"the open" is allowed to stand "opener," unveiling what was previously unseen,
allowing potentialities to actualize themselves. The Glucksman Gallery shows

this particularly clearly. Its landings allow the town's topography to be crossed in ways that not only open settings into one another but also let them withdraw into themselves. Put differently, its ways of arresting and initiating changes in level involve sideways reach and lateral differentiation. Landings in the Glucksman Gallery are the means by which the terrain is crossed and crossed out. Serving as instruments of spatial continuity, they are at the same time structural facts and social emblems that have achieved and express stability. Unmoving, they allow movement, the sort of movement that is both integrative and exploratory. Their *stability* is not only tectonic but temporal; like habits and institutions it is lasting.

Movement by means of landings goes against the concept of *flow*, which gets so much prominence in contemporary theorizing. Elsewhere I have discussed the fact that this image of movement is not new to architecture—already half a century ago George Howe described "flowing space" as "*the concept of our time*,"[1] and the so-called "fathers" of the modern movement, Frank Lloyd Wright, Theo van Doesburg, Mies van der Rohe, and Sigfried Giedion, asserted more or less the same thing. For them, and for many others since, flowing space represented the fundamental discovery of modern architecture, setting the stage for new patterns of life that were to be healthy and free. Nowadays flow can characterize virtually all aspects of a building: its spatial structure, iconography, "information," even its construction detailing (achieved by virtue of new software technologies). If the building is not to be a continuous ramp, however, it must have points from which movement begins and at which it ends: landings. The Glucksman Gallery acknowledges this principle not once or twice, but repeatedly, stopping and restarting passage for the sake of spatial definition and orientation.

Unlike pictorial space, the depth of which is always *ahead*, the depth of architecture is *all around*, exceeding any particular view, never just frontal, but equally lateral. In the early stages of project making, the single most important task is to understand the different characteristics of the site's wider milieu, for a basic function of the building is to serve as the means by which they cross over and into one another. The Glucksman Gallery stands at the edge of University College Cork. Its marginal position allows it to mediate many conditions, two of which are often seen in opposition: the campus and the town. The building's northward and westward prospects make its double orientation vividly clear. On its north side the building faces an urban landscape of great density. Just beyond the lawn that borders the gallery's ground-floor "river room" runs a garden path that rings the campus at its lowest level. The trees lining this walk rise above the gallery's upper decks and shade the river, a southern channel of the River Lee. Before the university was built, this branch of Cork's river flowed along a line further south, at the base of the present escarpment, having cut that cliff's footing before being redirected along its current track. On the opposite bank of the river's sixty-five-foot width stand the private yards and back facades of a row of houses, sheltered somewhat by fences and bushes. Further north, on the other side of the northern channel, the suburbs of Cork rise on the hills that enclose the entire town. From those summits in the distance, to the valley in which the gallery stands, the following elements cross in front of one another: a lawn, tree screen, river walk and river, backs and fronts of a housing terrace, a cross-town highway, remnants of an ancient dyke, another river, houses, and hills. These layers are not unapparent from the building, for its main axis or line of approach forms an exact perpendicular to all of them.

While the building's orientation toward the town is layered in depth, its prospect toward the center of the university opens onto a series of levels (platforms or terraces) stacked up to the height of the old university quadrangle. At right angles to the river room is the gallery's café, facing westward. Like a baroque *sala terrena*, it, too, opens onto the lawn that edges the building's base. When the café's glazed doors are slid sideways, the interior extends onto a wide deck, half shaded by the cantilevered galleries above. This "landing" leads to a green that is much wider than its northern counterpart, filling the entire space left by the ancient meander of the river. In the future, this lawn will display works of art, but now it is used as a park. Centuries of erosion have exposed the geological substrate of the mound on which the oldest parts of the university stand. Looking westward from the gallery, one sees a wall of limestone in the near distance, only partly screened by trees. A walkway up the slope leads to the university quadrangle, built in 1845 by Thomas Deane. Slightly further from the gallery, but a little lower than the quadrangle and closer to the river is a remnant of the county jail, built in 1818 as an extension to facilities constructed in the late eighteenth century. Well before then, before Queen Victoria's advisory committee proposed that an open site near the prison should be the location of Cork's new university, the summit had been the location of a monastery. Each of these levels has its counterpart in the gallery, as a look at the building's side elevation and section will show.

A small detail in the building's upper level is a remarkable example of this. The ground line at the base of the old quadrangle coincides exactly with the split between the upper and lower sections of the two-part windows in Gallery 1. A "deep section" (showing the building's interiors together with their exterior backdrop) reveals this coincidence very clearly. That there are windows in an art gallery is an interesting fact in itself. That the line of their division corresponds to a level in the distance is even more so. André Malraux's famous text *Museum Without Walls* was written in opposition to the enclosed sense of "art for its own sake" that had become common fifty years ago and the result of which might be called museums without openings. By rejecting the introverted and isolated qualities of most modern galleries, and engaging their building with the town, O'Donnell + Tuomey have opened the world of art into life.

The two-part windows bring to mind Kahn's Exeter Library. Like the differentiated apertures in the library, the lower part illuminates the interior locally, the upper part widely. Unlike Kahn's example, however, this split operates on different planes. The lower part is realized as a window wall that is rotated outward to face some point in the distance (the quadrangle in one case, the houses opposite the river in the other). Above, the glazing remains co-planar with the white wall. The space created by these crossing planes is balcony-like; it is part of the room but outside it. Placing a work of art, a piece of sculpture, for example, into this bay achieves a remarkable coordination of distances and contents. No longer are the landscape and town so far away and the work of art so close by—the first have entered the room's depth (as ambient light), and the second stands before spectators both in and outside the building. To find equivalent crossings at a building's edge one would have to turn to the better examples of baroque architecture. If marginal like a porch, the windows in the Glucksman Gallery also approximate the condition of a perch, by virtue of their hovering position. Porch or perch, they serve as stopping places (landings) along the path through the galleries that cross distances into one another.

Extending beyond the ramp that forms the main approach to the building, the large volume containing the galleries partly covers an open-air deck in front of the ground-level café. This deck, like the gallery "perch," crosses distinct settings into one another. Similar eateries can be found in most galleries and museums these days. Yet, this café is unlike most because of its marginal position and interconnectedness with settings outside the building. Obviously, it can be reached from within the gallery; in plan it is positioned diagonally opposite the river room, to the east of the landing at the base of the central stair. But when its full-height sliding doors are open, the café is also accessible from the campus walkway above, by means of a small stairway that parallels the entry ramp, and from the great lawn into which it reaches. If its deck is understood as a landing, the café can be seen to coordinate at least three crossings: the diagonal of public rooms at the building's base; a short-cut from the campus path to the river; or any wander across the lawn. This role would seem to make it open, like the deck above. But as a room, the café possesses all the qualities the forecourt landing lacks: darkness, depth, and limited horizontal extent; in other words, enclosure. Its contrast with the terrace above it is most apparent when seen from the lawn.

From a distance the café appears as a black hollow in the white mass of the building's base. Inhabited platforms are something of a commonplace in modern architecture; a few of the most well-known are Mies's New National Gallery in Berlin, Utzon's Sydney Opera House, and (closer in subject matter) the National Gallery on the Mound in the center of Edinburgh. This one conceals its contents more than those others, however, because of the very sharp contrast between its shadowed depth and the patterned flatness of the plinth. A closer look at the site's stone, as it stands out from the soil on the face of the escarpment, reveals the congeniality of the building's base with the land; for the cliff wall, too, has shadowed slices in the depths of its surface, and these, like the dark cut in the plinth, contrast with the white of the limestone. What is more, the bone-like stone gives a sense of permanence to both the base and the cliff. Like any example of the baroque *sala terrene*, the café's cross-overs into its vicinity are key to its character. Owned by neither the building nor the garden, the room belongs to both.

Apart from housing the café, the delivery, and service areas, the primary function of the building's broad base would seem to be support of the entry forecourt. Yet, because it ends both the ramp that descends from the campus path and the steps that rise from the river walk, this space can also be seen as a landing that is proportioned not to the gallery but its vicinity. When seen at this scale, and understood as part of the campus and town, not just the building, the forecourt stands between the two major lines of approach—the stair and ramp—as well as a number of minor ones: the short-cut from the campus path down to the café lawn; a second approach from lower down the campus path; and a small stair at the opposite corner of the plan that descends to the service yard to the west of the building.

Nothing in particular is made of the confluence of these routes; instead, the space seems happy to wait for events to occur, like a tray or table on which things are placed now and then, only to be removed at some later time. While nothing of the basilican monumentality of Kahn's courtyard at Salk characterizes this clearing, it exercises a similar restraint. A certain receptiveness is the result, which only serves to emphasize the forecourt's integrative function as the crossing of several routes and its role as a landing, the chief purpose of which is to *open toward* unforeseen conditions (Heaney's "February air"). As the architects have left it, the content of the space is not yet decided. Not only is movement paused but also meaning: while the forecourt reaches toward the various elements near it, it stops short of each of them, resisting their claims. Allowed to stand *beyond* the forecourt, the surrounding situations still show what existed *before* the landing stepped onto the site, actualizing history by coupling a topographical inheritance with an architectural possibility. If anything is staged on the deck it is a play of shadows across the dry grid, shadows cast by precisely those figures the landing keeps at a distance.

Deeply shaded by the galleries above, the entry hall's rich intensity sharply contrasts with the tacit spread of the forecourt. Despite its relative darkness (or maybe because of it, like a *camera obscura*) this setting is the most integrative of all the building's crossings, bringing within reach aspects of all that is around: the forecourt behind and the town ahead, the galleries above, and the river below. Here are also the main stair leading up to the galleries, an elevator, and a showcase straight ahead, which is as yet waiting for work to be installed. The reflections of leaves and clouds suffuse all of these places, as does the play of light they supply, quickening the qualities of the foyer's materials and transparencies. For comparison with a similarly synthetic (and shadowed) setting in modern architecture, one could turn to the foyer of Le Corbusier's Swiss Pavilion in Paris. In that case, as in this, entry confronts aspects or fragments of all the settings the building and its vicinity have to offer. But to build up content, Le Corbusier relies on images (in the photo murals, the display cases, and so on) much more than O'Donnell + Tuomey do. While the display of imagery makes his foyer rather enclosed, Le Corbusier also allowed the space to "leak" outside itself through lateral apertures, stairs, and landings. In the Cork Gallery, by contrast, the openings are hardly marginal. Through glazing on nearly all sides, aspects of the surroundings emerge frontally and obliquely, at varying distances and elevations.

A decisive aspect of the gallery's landings and crossings, and of the one at the entry in particular, is their sense of freedom. Freedom in this context means more than just the modernist "flow," the goal of achieving an absence of "external" limitations to allow for movement that is independent, sovereign, or autarkic. The freedom I would like to evoke here is not of movement but of the object, not unrestricted passage through the interior's several settings, but independence from the constraints of the inherited context—the city being the most restrictive of contexts. Of course, there are both conceptual and practical problems with this conception of freedom. When it attempts a categorical separation from its vicinity, the building cuts itself off from the very conditions that grant it its reality and identity. Sovereignty in architecture cannot mean unconditional independence, for no building can stand apart from its context. Buildings are created out of materials that are available or brought to a location, they are built with labor practices that are common or possible there, they depend on social patterns, natural and civic ecologies, cultural memories and aspirations, and so on. The freedom they express— the freedom of their stance—can only be understood *within* these conditions. The identity of a building does not result from absolute sameness with others in its vicinity, nor from absolute difference, but degrees of both. In the absence of a background no figure could appear—the first presupposes the second against which it shows itself. It is precisely this dependence of the figure on its ground that suggests another sense of the building's freedom, a freedom that arises out of the conditions that are given to design, not apart from them.

The freedom that characterizes the entry to the Glucksman Gallery lies in its function as a place for well-informed decision making. No decision is more difficult than the one made in absence of understanding, nor is any such choice really meaningful. Self-determination occurs through decisions that are taken *in the midst* of circumstances, particularly conflicting circumstances. The paradoxical term "freestanding participation" aptly describes this *allocentric* situation, which applies to the gallery as a whole, and its entry in particular. The task of the entry space is to draw together the several opportunities presented by the ambient circumstances and offer them to movement as a context of choice. The more the differences of the surrounding's various situations are made apparent, the more significant will be the choice of one or another. Herein lies the freedom that we experience in this space. Buildings do not sustain autonomy by divorcing themselves from "external constraints" but by using those very limitations as a framework for action.

While the gallery's engagement with its topography is apparent in its entry space, this interweaving is equally clear in its elevations. In the history of art, figures that are torn between several alternative, equally attractive choices are often depicted as experiencing an internal conflict that has an impact on their physical composition. In mannerist and baroque painting and sculpture, they are known as *contrapposto* figures and have a number of typical characteristics. The first is that they display aspects of the figure's front and back sides simultaneously. A second and analogous characteristic is an opposition between the way the figure faces (or looks) and reaches. There is a wonderful drawing by Michelangelo for the *Battle of Cascina* that shows a single figure extending itself in four or five directions: one leg pointing to the left, another straight downwards, the waist facing forward, the head twisted completely round to the rear, and an arm extending to the right—a figure truly *engaged* in battle, torn one might say in different directions. In this case, and in similar designs, contrary movements lead to a third characteristic of *contrapposto* composition: axial disequilibrium. The equivalent (structural) principle in architecture would be asymmetrical balance, kept in static equilibrium by means of cantilevers.

The formal properties of these figures are not what I want to stress, however, for the free-standing work is always only half the real story. When describing Gianlorenzo Bernini's sculpture of David, Rudolph Wittkower suggested that the "spiritual focus of the statue [presumably Goliath] is outside the statue itself," in the space we also occupy. To understand the work, Wittkower suggests we must de-center the figure, we need to realize that its center, or centers exist outside it, in the field of the battle, or more generally, on the horizon.

David Summers, in his account of *contrapposto* observed that the aim of "counter-positioning" was to use variety to give the sense of movement, for nothing brought the work to life as much as movement. But the key is that the movement of a body, or any of its parts is always toward or away from some attractive or repulsive figure within its milieu: the figure comes to life, or defines itself by taking a stand for or against conditions outside itself. Both axial disequilibrium, which allows the simultaneous appearance of front and back, and reaching in opposite directions are prompted by conditions outside the body. A figure's profile—an architectural elevation is what I have in mind—indicates the choices it has made in the midst of the circumstances that surround it. Its decisions also define its character. Put differently, freedom, as described above, finds its foothold in a context of antithetical surroundings—the sort that can be found in just about any urban situation. There is no other way of understanding the Glucksman Gallery's *contrapposto* profile; it is irregular, distended, even convulsive, by virtue of being engaged in the contraries of its vicinity.

Given the interest the building shows in the many aspects of its surrounds, it may seem sensible to describe it as a kind of nexus or knot that binds together and concentrates the community of routes that cross its property. This image only applies, however, as long as it does not involve a sense of centrality, in the magnetic meaning of that word, for the building, at least the landing at the mid-point of its main axis, is more like a junction than a gathering point. What is more, it is not only planimetric but a spatial or volumetric intersection. A good way to think of it is to imagine a Loosian *raumplan* made fully topographical. Many critics have characterized Loos's *raumplan* designs as internal configurations, severed from their topographical frame of reference, although the building's apertures reveal linkage between inside and out. In the case of the Glucksman Gallery, however, the interconnections that Loos condensed onto the building's skin are prolonged into the reach of its volumes, toward the external situations they seek to engage. This is why its pattern of distribution can be called an *allocentric* order—centered outside itself.

The forecourt landing of the Glucksman Gallery is a place where aspects of the extended topography cross over and into one another. At no point on this level does any part show itself fully. Standing on the forecourt, the stair within the entry hall is obvious, but seen darkly, under the shadow cast by the galleries above. The same obscurity blankets the showcase, but it receives light from the sky above the river. No vantage can be taken that would isolate any of these parts from the others. Inclusions, on the other hand, are many: leaves and clouds are included in the gallery's "balcony" window; the face of the town behind the campus entry looks over the wide rim of the forecourt; the column that partially limits the café below is among those that line the opposite side of the wide deck. Experience is not offered single objects but aspects of many, not items side by side, but a field, a landscape, or topography whose depth is structured by the mutual envelopment of things. Within such a horizon, no room, court, or lawn appears whole and complete in itself, but always partially blocked by and blocking others. This is because each plunges its roots into the midst of its world as the site and soil of its unique divergence. Nor is the famous figure-background stable, as the two exchange roles depending on perceptual and practical interests, and the margins they share lead to reciprocal co-mingling and infiltration.

In every project there is the site, and there are the building's settings. The first is given and the second are designed. No truism in architecture is more obvious. But the configuration and posture of the Glucksman Gallery show that the reality of the building is not comprehended by this postulate. Each of the two—the site and the setting—crosses into the other in such a fashion that the limit between them is as indeterminate as it is incontestable. Each of the rooms in this building makes allusions to others nearby and far away—that much is clear. Less obvious but even more important is the realization that each constitutes itself as a room by virtue of these allusions. Thus, the gallery's most radical lesson is that project making is not limited to determination but requires a specifically architectural sort of indetermination, a disintegration of the object that promotes the slippage of settings into one another, resulting in a configuration of both kinships and differences, as in a family. In other words, the task taken up in the design of this building was not the definition of forms but the orchestration of relationships.

In architecture, depth is a phenomenon of congeniality in the etymological sense of that word: of like, common, or kindred origin. The congenial depth of the Glucksman Gallery is at once inviting and challenging. John Tuomey once used the term "strangely familiar" to name its remote immediacy. If, indeed, the building crosses paths by crossing out their individuality, the aim and result of its work stands as an emblem of what was otherwise unseen but integral about the world in which it stands.

[1] David Leatherbarrow, *Uncommon Ground: Architecture, Technology, and Topography* (Cambridge, Mass.: M.I.T. Press, 2002), 176–80.

Project Credits and Awards

Irish Pavilion
11 Cities/11 Nations Exhibition, Leeuwarden, the
    Netherlands, 1990
Irish Museum of Modern Art, Kilmainham, Dublin,
    Ireland, 1991
Building area: 1,075 square feet
Architects: Collaboration Brian Maguire / O'Donnell +
    Tuomey
Structural engineers: Fearon O'Neill Rooney
Lighting design: Shiu Kay Kan
General contractors: FÁS Trainees
AAI Downes Medal (Premier Award)

Three Buildings in Temple Bar (1992–1996)
Temple Bar, Dublin, Ireland
UIA Abercrombie prize for urban design (Group 91)

Irish Film Centre (1992)
Building area: 19,375 square feet
Architects: O'Donnell + Tuomey
Structural engineers: Fearon O'Neill Rooney
Mechanical engineers: Engineering Design Associates
General contractors: Cleary and Doyle
RIAI Award
AAI Downes Medal
Andrea Palladio International Award Finalist
Sunday Times Building of the Year Award Joint First Prize

National Photographic Archive (1992)
Building area: 16,465 square feet
Architects: O'Donnell + Tuomey / Group 91
Structural engineers: Muir Associates
Mechanical engineers: JV Tierney
General contractors: P. Rogers and Sons
AAI Award

Gallery of Photography (1996)
Building area: 3,450 square feet
Architects: O'Donnell + Tuomey / Group 91
Structural engineers: Muir Associates
Mechanical engineers: JV Tierney
General contractors: P. Rogers and Sons
AAI Downes Medal (Premier Award)

Blackwood Golf Centre (1994)
Clandeboye, County Down, Northern Ireland
Building area: 8,600 square feet
Architects: O'Donnell + Tuomey
Structural engineers: Armstrong and Shaw
Mechanical engineers: Buckley and Downie
General contractors: Felix O'Hare
RIBA Award
RIAI Award
RIAI Gold Medal, commendation

Hudson House (1998)
Navan, County Meath, Ireland
Building area: 1,185 square feet
Architects: O'Donnell + Tuomey
General contractors: Warnock Brothers
RIAI Award
AAI Award
Irish Concrete Society, special commendation

Ranelagh Multidenominational School (1998)
Ranelagh, Dublin, Ireland
Building area: 12,375 square feet
Architects: O'Donnell + Tuomey
Structural engineers: Fearon O'Neill Rooney
Mechanical engineers: JV Tierney
General contractors: Pierce Healy
RIBA Award—Stirling Prize finalist
*RIBA Award for best building in Educational Category in
    Europe*
RIAI Triennial Gold Medal Winner, 1998–2000
RIAI Award
AAI Downes Award (Premier Award)
Mies Van der Rohe Award for European Architecture, finalist

Furniture College Letterfrack (2001)
Letterfrack, County Galway, Ireland
Building area: new 28,525 square feet / existing 14,692
square feet
Architects: O'Donnell + Tuomey
Structural engineers: Chris Southgate
Mechanical engineers: McArdle McSweeney
General contractors: Purcell Construction
RIBA Award
RIAI Award
AAI Downes Medal (Premier Award)
Mies Van der Rohe Award for European Architecture, Finalist

Social Housing in Galbally (2002)
Galbally, County Limerick, Ireland
Building area: 9,050 square feet
Architects: O'Donnell + Tuomey
Structural engineers: Michael Punch
General contractors: Kyle Civil Engineering Ltd.
RIBA Award
RIAI Award
AAI Award

Leinster House Press Reception Room (2002)
Leinster House, Dublin, Ireland
Building area: 1,075 square feet
Architects: O'Donnell + Tuomey
Structural engineers: O'Connor Sutton Cronin
Mechanical engineers: Environmental Design
Partnership
General contractors: Brock + Sons
RIAI Award
AAI Award

Lyric Theater (2003–2007)
Belfast, Northern Ireland
Building area: 46,285 square feet
Architects: O'Donnell + Tuomey

Medical Research Laboratory (2003)
University College Dublin, Ireland
Building area: 14,000 square feet
Architects: O'Donnell + Tuomey
Structural engineers: Arup
Mechanical engineers: Arup
General contractors: Townlink Construction
RIBA Award
RIAI Award
AAI Award

Howth House (2003)
Howth, County Dublin, Ireland
Building area: 3,000 square feet
Architects: O'Donnell + Tuomey
Structural engineers: Downes Associates
General contractors: Hillside Contracts
RIBA Award

Ireland's Pavilion at the Venice Biennale (2004)
Venice, Italy
Building area: 4,300 square feet
Architects: O'Donnell + Tuomey
Structural engineers: Chris Southgate
General contractors: Timber Structures of Ireland
RIAI Award

Glucksman Gallery (2004)
University College Cork, Ireland
Building area: 24,750 square feet
Architects: O'Donnell + Tuomey
Structural engineers: Horgan Lynch
Mechanical engineers: Arup
General contractors: Hegarty Instruction
RIBA Award—Stirling Prize finalist
RIAI Award Best Public Building of the Year

Biography

Sheila O'Donnell
Born Dublin 1953
B.Arch. University College Dublin 1976
Spence and Webster, London 1978–80
MA RCA Royal College of Art, London 1980
Colquhoun and Miller, London 1979–80
Stirling Wilford and Associates, London 1980–81
Studio lecturer, University College Dublin 1981–present
Visiting critic, Princeton University 1987
Architecture and Culture Conference Venezuela 1993
External examiner, Manchester 1996–1998, Cambridge 2000–2002
Fellow of the Royal Institute of Architects of Ireland 1994

John Tuomey
Born Tralee 1954
B.Arch. University College Dublin 1976
Stirling Wilford Associates, London 1976–80
Office of Public Works, Dublin 1981–87
Studio lecturer University College Dublin 1980–present
Visiting critic, Princeton University 1987, 1993
Visiting design critic, GSD Harvard 1988–89
External examiner, Architectural Association 1988–94, Cambridge 1993–98,
Oxford 1993, UEL 1996–98
President Architectural Association of Ireland 1992–93
Fellow of the Royal Institute of Architects of Ireland 1994
M.Arch. University College Dublin 2004

Exhibitions

1986	Figurative Architecture, AA London / IFA Paris / Municipal Gallery Dublin
1988	Currents, Projects by John Tuomey, GSD Harvard
1988	Collaboration: The Pillar Project, GPO Dublin
1990	11 Cities / 11 Nations, Leeuwarden, the Netherlands, Irish Pavilion
1991	Irish Museum of Modern Art (IMMA), Irish Pavillion
1991	Making a Modern Street: an Urban Proposal, Architecure Forum Zurich / IMMA Dublin
1996	RIAI Building on the Edge of Europe, A Survey of Contemporary Architecture in Ireland
1997	20th Century Ireland, Deutsches Architektur Museum Frankfurt / Royal Hibernian Academy Dublin
1997	O'Donnell + Tuomey, 10 Years Work, RIAI Architecture Center Dublin
1998	Academy without Walls, Royal Hibernian Academy, Dublin
2000	European Panoramas, Pavillion de l'Arsenal, Paris
2002	New Trends of Architecture in Europe and Japan, Art Front Gallery, Tokyo
2003	Tulca Festival, "Architecture at the Edge," Galway
2004	9th International Architecture Exhibition, Venice Biennale, Ireland's Pavilion
2005	Architecture, Craft and Culture, Recent work by O'Donnell + Tuomey, DESSA Gallery, Ljubljana
	New Trends of Architecture in Europe and Asia, Crawford Gallery, Cork (exhibition installation by O'Donnell + Tuomey)

Competitions

Temple Bar Framework Plan, Group 91, Invited, First Prize, 1992
Blackwood Golf Centre, Invited, First Prize, 1992
Walsall Art Gallery, Walsall, England, 1996
Cambridge Arts Cinema, Cambridge, England, Invited, 1997
Limavady Arts Centre, Limavady, Northern Ireland, Second Prize, 1998
National Centre for Film and Drama, University College Dublin, Invited, First Prize, 1999
Medical Research Laboratory University College Dublin, Invited, First Prize, 1999
Pearse Street Development Plan, Trinity College Dublin, Invited, First Prize, 2002
Lincoln Arts Centre, Lincoln, UK, Invited, Second Prize, 2003
Lyric Theatre, Belfast, Northern Ireland, First Prize, 2003
An Gaelaras Cultural Centre, Derry, Northern Ireland, First Prize, 2004
Royal Shakespeare Theatre, Stratford, UK, Second Prize, 2005
Aberdeen Library, University of Aberdeen, Scotland, Invited, Second Prize, 2005

List of Works

1989	Lighthouse Cinema Dublin
1991	Irish Pavilion, Irish Museum of Modern Art, Dublin
1992	Irish Film Centre, Temple Bar, Dublin
	Murtagh House, County Dublin
	Temple Bar Framework Plan, Group 91, 1994
	Blackwood Golf Centre, Clandeboye, County Down, Northern Ireland
1996	Good Shepherd, Satellite Campus University College Cork, Cork, Ireland, project
	National Photographic Archive, Temple Bar, Dublin 2
	Gallery of Photography, Temple Bar, Dublin 2
1998	Hudson House, Navan, County Meath, Ireland
	Ranelagh Multidenominational School, Ranelagh, Dublin 6
2001	Furniture College, Letterfrack, County Galway, Ireland
2002	Kindercluster, Waterwin, Leidsche Rijn, Utrecht, the Netherlands
	Zuidpoort, Delft, the Netherlands
	Social Housing, Galbally, County Limerick, Ireland
	Martin House, Blackrock, County Louth, Ireland
	Milkbar, Montague Street, Dublin
	Druid Theatre, Galway, Co Galway, Project
2003	Howth House, County Dublin
	Medical Research Laboratory, University College Dublin
	Milkbar II, Setanta Place, Dublin
2004	Lewis Glucksman Gallery, University College Cork
	Ireland's Pavilion, International Architectural Biennale, Venice, Italy
2005	Work in Progress
	Houses
	Killiney House, County Dublin, Ireland
	Gray House, County Dublin, Ireland
	Strand House, Rosslare, County Wexford

Selected Bibliography

Monographs

Kester Rattenbury, *Archaeology of the Air. O'Donnell + Tuomey, Architecture.* Trieste: Navado Press, 2004.

John Tuomey, *Architecture, Craft and Culture.* Kinsale: Gandon Editions, 2004.

O'Donnell + Tuomey Architects, *Transformation of an Institution,* The Furniture College, Letterfrack. Kinsale: Gandon Editions, 2004.

O'Donnell + Tuomey, *Building and Projects.* Kinsale: Gandon Editions, 1998.

Brian Maguire and O'Donnell + Tuomey, *The Irish Pavilion.* Kinsale: Gandon Editions, 1992.

Books

The Phaidon Atlas of Contemporary World Architecture. (Featured projects: Ranelagh Multidenominational School, Centre for Research into Infectious Diseases, Letterfrack Furniture College, Galbally Social Housing) New York: Phaidon, 2004.

Deyan Sudjic, *10x10_2 100 Architects 10 Critics.* (Featured projects: Howth House, Galbally Social Housing, Glucksman Gallery, Centre for Research into Infectious Diseases) New York: Phaidon, 2005.

Dejan Sudjic, *Home, The Twentieth-Century House.* (Featured project: Hudson House) London: Laurence King Publishing, 1999.

Kester Ratterbury / Kieran Long, *Architects Today.* (Featured projects: Furniture College Letterfrack, Irish Pavilion, Gallery of Photography, National Photographic Archive) London: Laurence King Publishing, 2004.

Hugh Pearman, *Contemporary World Architecture.* (Featured project: Blackwood Golf Centre) New York: Phaidon, 2002.

Jeffrey Myerson, *New Public Architecture.* London: Laurence King Publishing, 1996.

Dietmar Steiner, *New Building Today, European Architecture of the 1990's.* (Featured projects: Irish Pavilion, Irish Film Centre) Basel: Birkhauser Verlag, 1995.

Annette Becker, John Olley, and Wilfred Wang, *20th-Century Architecture Ireland.* (Featured projects: Temple Bar, Irish Film Centre, Gallery of Photography, Blackwood Golf Centre) Munich: Prestel Verlag, 1997.

Periodicals

Architecture Magazine

  Greg Delaney, "Life of the Party" (December 2005)

Architecture + Urbanism

  "Architects' Offices" (January 2006)

  "New University Buildings, Lewis Glucksman Gallery, University College Cork" (February 2005)

  Hera Van Sande, "Eight Architects in Ireland," Furniture College Letterfrack (October 2003)

  "Wooden Buildings, Irish Pavilion" (May 1998)

Architectural Review

  "O'Donnell + Tuomey, Theatre, Belfast, UK" (April 2005)

  Jeremy Till, "Effortless Artistry" (August 2005)

  "Irish Reels" (January 1993)

Baumeister 8

  "Ireland, O'Donnell+Tuomey" (August 2005)

Casabella 730

  Pietro Valle, "The Multiplication of Identity" (February 2005)

Icon

  "Venice Architecture Biennale" (November 2004)

Domus

  Deyan Sudjic, "Academic Sciences" (October 2003)

  "Group 91 Renovation of the Temple Bar Urban District in Dublin" (November 1998)

  "Golf Centre, Clandeboye, Ireland" (April 1996)

Archi 8

  Kenneth Frampton, "Abbotstown/Furniture College Letterfrack" (April 2001)

Quaderns 226

  "Hudson House"

Architecture Magazine

  "Brick-and-Mortar Modern." (August 1999)

Collaborators (since 1988)

Nicki Brock
Harriet Browne
Lorraine Bull
Elizabeth Burns
Peter Carroll
Willie Carey
Susie Carson
Sorcha Coleman
Susan Cogan
Charlotte Curry
Will Dimond
Marcus Donaghy
Kevin Donovan
Rebecca Egan
Jeana Gearty
Ailbhe Gerrard
Morwenna Gerrard
Linda Hartsema
Richard Jeffrey

Jens Kuchenmeister
Clodagh Latimer
Jitka Leonard
Jim Luke
My Lundblad
Fiona McDonald
Sean Mahon
Andrew Morrison
Tom O'Donnell
Emma O'Neill
Thomas Pickert
Adam Richards
Beatrix Schmidt
Lisa Shell
Triona Stack
Conor Sreenan
Gavin Wheatley